I Hate Whining Except When I'm Doing It

I Hate Whining Except When I'm Doing It

AND OTHER LESSONS LEARNED AT MY CHILDREN'S KNEES

SHEILA RABE

Christian Publications
CAMP HILL, PENNSYLVANIA

Christian Publications, Inc.
3825 Hartzdale Drive
Camp Hill, PA 17011
www.cpi-horizon.com
www.christianpublications.com

Faithful, biblical publishing since 1883

I Hate Whining Except When I'm Doing It
ISBN: 0-87509-645-X

LOC Control Number: 96-86344

© 1996 by Christian Publications, Inc.

Printed in the United States of America

00 01 02 03 04   6 5 4 3 2

Cover illustration by Ron Wheeler

CONTENTS

Mom's Lessons in Philosophy

Perspective

Perspective, Advanced Course

Principles of Change

AUTHOR'S NOTE

The main characters (and what characters they are!) in this book are obviously not fictional. Only the names have been changed to protect the guilty. My children and husband have graciously let me lay bare their faults as well as my own, and I'm grateful.

Since the lessons in this primer are grouped topically, they aren't always chronological. But since the books of the Bible aren't assembled sequentially, I figure I'm in good company and that you'll forgive me.

Again, my thanks to my kids for letting me make examples of them. They're good sports, great kids and they love the Lord. What more could a parent ask?

ABOUT HIGHER EDUCATION

My parents taught me the basics for survival: "Don't touch"; "Hot!"; "Look both ways before crossing the street"; "Use your deodorant."

They also taught me manners: "Don't talk with your mouth full." And respect: "Don't talk to your mother like that, especially with your mouth full!"

And they helped me form good habits, such as going to church and Sunday school and doing my work before I played instead of afterward.

My next arena of learning was in school, years and years of it. In my early years I gobbled information and spat it back when my teachers required. In college I stepped beyond that and learned to think. (The thinking wasn't always very clear, but just seeing the process start probably gave my parents hope.)

From parachurch organizations and my church

I learned God's Word. I received an overview of the Bible and learned about its history.

My parents nurtured me. My college professors taught me to think. My pastors and various Bible teachers impacted me and helped me grow spiritually. But some of the most important lessons of my life I learned right in the unprivacy of my own home, the Holy Spirit often using my own children, Dolly, Honey and Junior (yes, the names are changed!) as unwitting teachers.

As they grew I watched their often immature and rebellious behavior and saw myself as God sees me. As I have disciplined and counseled my children, God has often taught me through my words to them.

My relationships with my children mirror my relationship with my heavenly Father. Often, the reflection is not a pretty sight. I've disgustedly watched two-year-old children throw tantrums, only to realize I can be equally disgusting. I hate whining—except when I'm doing it. I firmly believe in discipline—for others. My children often drive me up the wall. And while I try to cope with their behavior, God deals with mine, saying, "Do you see similarities? Do you need to work on the same thing as your children?"

In the laboratory of love, my husband has innocently helped me mix many a Molotov cocktail. Usually, not until after the explosion do I learn what went wrong.

My lessons have been basic, dealing with facts I've known since I was ten. One at a time, I've learned to personally apply precepts which I had previously considered only in general, non-threatening terms. Those verses I recited as a child moved from head information to lifestyle as my spiritual home schooling progressed.

I'm a little embarrassed to admit this, but I learned some of my most important lessons at my children's knees. Thank God for kids.

MOM'S LESSONS IN BEHAVIORAL SCIENCE

I always thought behavioral science involved rats lost in a maze. It was simply a class that brainy, skinny boys took in college. It was a job for men with gray, frizzy hair and white lab coats, which dealt with scientific principles and teaching Russian wolfhounds when to come for dinner. It certainly wasn't anything I was interested in.

Until the day my Father decided my behavior needed some modification. Then we started lessons in behavioral science.

TIME
MANAGEMENT

Chapter 1

Diary of a Mad Housewife

Wednesday morning, 1987, 8:39 a.m, in a tan rambler style home on Forty-second Avenue, somewhere in suburbia:

Dolly is already safely loaded onto her wheelchair bus and is on her way to school. One down, two to go. Junior and Honey have eaten breakfast and their lunches are packed.

Honey is in the bathroom, primping her hair, a newly acquired interest. (If she would only consider bathing once in awhile. . . . But that may be asking too much of a fifth grader.) Junior is raring to go. At first grade, he has not yet felt the thrill of school wear off. He's in his coat, waiting for his sister by the front door and talking at me. I'm reading a book and occasionally nod my head so he'll think I'm listening.

The book capturing my attention is about the adventures of three Australian women, and it's *so* good! I picked it up early this morning to read for just a couple of minutes. By now my recreational reading has extended into my devotion time and way beyond but never mind. I'll have my devotions after the kids are off to school.

Suddenly a distant rumbling quickly grows into a roar. The sound penetrates my fantasy world and I spring off the couch like I've been shot from a cannon. "Quick, Junior, there's the school bus!" I shout, yanking open the front door. Junior tears out the door and dashes for the bus. "Honey!" I bellow, "Come on. Now! You've got to go!"

I hear the thunder of feet running down the hall from bathroom to bedroom, then nothing. *What is that child doing? She'll miss the bus!* I storm down the hall to my daughter's room. Honey is struggling to put on her tenny-runners. So far, she's only wearing one. The bus waits at the corner bus stop. How many seconds will it take to load ten kids? I yank my daughter to her feet and hand her the other shoe. "Here! You'll have to run in your sock. Where's your lunch?"

"In the kitchen. "

"Where's your homework?" Silly question. It's scattered all over her bedroom floor.

The battle is lost. I'll never get this kid to the bus stop on time. I grab the shoe from my daughter's hand and throw it on the floor.

"This should never have happened!" I rant. "If you hadn't been in the bathroom primping! You knew you only had a few minutes until the school bus came. Now I have to take you to school." I stomp off in search of my own shoes.

Why are you really angry? asks a voice at the back of my mind.

"Because I have to run this kid to school and my morning will be shot," I mumble.

And?

"The day will be shot," I repeat hysterically.

It's only a half hour out of your day.

That was true. So why was I so angry?

I was mad because I knew I would have to pay for my early morning pleasures and I didn't want to. I'd already postponed my devotions as well as some routine morning chores. Taking my daughter to school would put me further behind, and I would spend the rest of the day playing catch-up, a no-win game. The morning was spinning out of control and I was sure I would have no time to do what I had wanted to do that afternoon.

That was why I was really upset. I would lose my pleasant afternoon. Like a toddler denied a breakable item, I felt thwarted. And I didn't like it.

Aren't you really taking your anger out on the wrong person? the voice suggested again.

I tried to think I wasn't, but deep down where I didn't want to look, I knew that I was, indeed, fingering the wrong girl for this mess. Of course, Honey should have been more organized. But as her mother, my job was to check on her. Children often have no concept of schedules so I was unfair to expect my daughter to have mastered such a theory. In fact, considering my own disregard for time, my expectations were ridiculous. ("Let me get the speck out of your eye, dear daughter, but disregard the two-by-four in mine.") I couldn't get around it. My anger with my daughter was really just a selfish tantrum.

Wednesday morning, 8:45 a.m.:

Mother and child walk out of their house to the car. I am wearing what all well-dressed suburban housewives with tardy daughters will wear this year: a fuzzy bathrobe, tennis shoes and a frown. My daughter's face is similarly adorned.

We enter the car and drive in silence. Finally, I murmur those painful two words. "I'm sorry. I'm sorry about a lot of things."

Wednesday morning, 9:10 a.m.:

A cream-colored station wagon pulls into the driveway of a tan rambler somewhere in suburbia. I get out of the car and go inside the house. I go to my bedroom, get my Bible off the nightstand and flip it open to a psalm. I'm looking for something I can read quickly, a token offering to ease my conscience. I read aloud, "My voice shalt thou hear in the morning O LORD; in the morning will I direct my prayer unto thee, and will look up" (Psalm 5:3, KJV).

I vow to make better use of my time tomorrow.

* * *

So, a few years later, how is Mom doing? Has she learned her lesson?

I think perhaps I have. And I've seen a definite correlation between training my daughter to get going in the morning and training myself. Getting Honey moving involves practical steps. Getting me off to my morning quiet time with the Father requires the same steps:

1. Put Honey and Mom to bed early enough for a good night's sleep.

I can't get my daughter going in the morning if she hasn't slept for a good eight hours the night before. I'm the same way. So to have time with my heavenly Father before the day begins, I have to bag the late night news. At exactly 10 o'clock I shut my book, turn off the light and close my eyes. If a classic old movie is showing on TV that I'd like to see, I videotape it for a Friday night, when I can stay up later.

2. Once the alarm rings Mom and Honey need to get up right away.

The light goes on in Honey's room, the covers go off and I make sure she's up and staggering before I leave her on her own and I usually succomb.

As for me? At the first sound of the alarm I roll out of the bed. Literally. If I have to crawl on the floor for a while to wake up, so be it.

For me, lying in bed after I awaken is an impossible dream. The warm covers tempt me to stay.

"A little sleep, a little slumber, a little folding of the hands to rest." That proverb (24:33) refers to the philosophy of the lazy man. He procrastinates, he postpones. "I'll weed my field tomorrow," he says. ". . . and poverty will come on you like a bandit" (24:34), says the wise man. The woman who postpones tending to her spiritual field soon finds herself spiritually poor.

If I suspect I'll have trouble getting up in the morning, I tell my husband, "Don't let me sleep!" He's always happy to oblige. Mr. Misery loves company. He figures if he has to be awake and struggling with a new day, so should I. The few times I've let him go to work, assuring him, "I'll get up in a few minutes," I've slept away two hours of my day.

3. Once up, Honey and Mom must ignore distractions.

In the fifth grade, Honey loved to play with the cat, read Nancy Drew mysteries, pick lint from her toes. . . . She liked to do anything but the steps necessary to get out the door for school. Now she's in high school, and little has changed except that Nancy Drew has stepped aside for cats who see red, eat Danish pastry and talk to cardinals. Oh, and of course the toe thing. Now she's busy flipping tapes in and out of her cassette player.

This still makes me crazy, but as I have worked with Honey I've noticed similarities in my own morning behavior. I am as easily distracted as my daughter. To get to my Bible, I must ignore the many calls of the house: the half-read newspaper from the previous night (it will just take a minute to finish this), kitchen clutter (I'll feel better with this out of the way), that unfinished mystery (just one chapter). I must ignore them all.

As soon as my husband's lunch is made and he's out the door, I go to my corner by the heater and meet with the Father. I can tidy the kitchen clutter and newspaper after the kids are up. But I can never recapture that early morning silence. I have to grab it before bodies stir and cupboards crash, before the phone rings and the demands of the day squeeze in on me.

Since I've started working outside the home, moving in the morning has become more important. If I don't start the day with the Lord, I know I won't get any special time with Him. The rest of my day gallops away, and at night I'm too tired.

Other women schedule different slots for quiet time. One friend who's a homemaker and professional seamstress prefers to work in the morning. At noon she stops for lunch and has her spiritual meal as well. She reads Scripture and takes a walk. Away from the distractions of the house, she can think about that Scripture and pray.

For the woman with babies and an upside-down schedule, quiet time can be even harder to find. But doing so is still possible—like when baby is having his bottle, taking his nap or nursing. What better time to pray for that little one, and to pray for the wisdom to nurture him, than when the house is still and the baby is cradled in your arms for that early morning feeding?

And speaking of the early morning, I think of my friend who was nightly awakened by her husband's nocturnal rumblings. She says she spent years praying God would cure her husband of his snoring so she could sleep. One night she realized maybe God didn't want her to sleep. In fact, maybe He was waking her up. She got out of bed and prayed. Now she spends a lot of pre-dawn time praying and searching Scripture. She says this time is so meaningful that she wouldn't trade it for sleep if she could.

Jesus commanded us to seek God's kingdom first. That means each day. If I'm too busy from the moment I awaken to spend time with God, whose kingdom am I seeking? Even if I spend the entire day doing good works for Him, what does it mean if I don't want to be with Him?

Like Pavlov's dogs, I need to associate ringing bells with food. In this case the ringing bell is my alarm clock, the food the Bread of Life. Hear the bell, Mom? It's time to get up and eat. Bon appétit!

Chapter 2

———

Busy Hands Are Frantic Hands

Proverbs 24:30-34

Apples simmered on the stove. Clean jars lined the counter, waiting to be filled with applesauce. Three large boxes of apples sat on the kitchen floor. I stood amid this mess, washing, cutting, stirring.

Junior, in the toddler stage, was "helping." He was so busy! He would take an apple from one box and deliver it to another. Then he would remove an apple from that second box and put it in yet another box.

I chuckled and thought, *Isn't that cute? He's so busy. And in his baby mind he thinks he is doing something important. Funny. He reminds me of someone I know. . . .*

That someone was me, running from activity to activity. A PTO meeting here, a committee meeting there. Now it's time for my writing class. Tomorrow night is church choir practice after I have two afternoon appointments. Saturday is my songwriter's critique group. Yesterday I said I'd help plan the Welcome Wagon's annual spring luncheon and style show. . . .

Busy hands are happy hands, right? Then let's get a little happier. Run here, run there. See me running everywhere.

One day I found I'd run out of breath and couldn't do all those important things. Suddenly I wasn't happy any more. And neither was my family.

The kids knew they had a mother. Their father fondly remembered her. "Yes, she had brown hair. Nice eyes, too. She was fun. There she goes, children, driving down the street. I think she's off to . . . Let me check. It's Wednesday. She's gone to choir practice."

After that sighting the kids began to look for Mom. Other Mommy sightings were reported but could not be confirmed—by the time a child dragged someone to the spot where Mom had been seen, she had rushed somewhere else. "I tell you, I saw her. Right there. Loading clothes in the dryer."

"How do you know it was her? Did you see her face?"

"No. But I recognized her voice when she said, 'Not now, I'm busy.' She was here, I tell you!"

I kept running faster, finding more things to do—all of them important. A friend told me to slow down and cut some things out of my life.

"I can't cut out anything," I insisted. "Everything I'm doing is important."

He looked like he didn't believe me.

I believed me. Until I got sick. Not the kind of sick where my family feared for my life, just sick enough to be couch-bound for a couple of weeks.

Once down, I looked around me. I saw my friend, Vonda, a high-energy, multi-talented overachiever, suddenly drop everything and go to a health farm to rest for three weeks. Another friend complained that stress was killing her. One friend bragged about her crazy schedule. Did I ever brag? Come to think of it, I did.

I remembered the two New Testament sisters, Mary and Martha. Contemplating Christ's words to Martha in Luke 10:41-42, I decided I spent much time on second rate things.

Why? Probably for the same reason Martha fussed over the dinner for Jesus. Probably for the same reason my friend bragged about her full schedule. I wanted to be important and needed. And anyway, so many things needed attention. Who could do them better than me?

Honestly, nearly anyone would have been better at some of those things. Atilla the Hun's mother would have made a more patient school health room volunteer ("You're not sick. Go back to class!"). And my lack of organizational skills hardly qualified me to be secretary in a women's club ("I'd love to read the minutes from last month's meeting, but I can't find them").

Then there was the time I directed "German Day" at the small German church where my husband and I served. I was full of ideas. But by the end of the celebration, several members of the church board probably had some ideas too—about what they'd like to do to me!

Entertainment for "German Day" was the first disaster. I got a painful case of telephone ear trying to find a German oompah band. Unfortunately, every oompah band from here to Munich was booked for that day.

"OK, the oompah band is out, but I've got a line on a great husband-and-wife duo!" I said. The duo idea failed. Next we were down to a strolling accordian player who cancelled at the last minute. We played records.

Publicity was another challenge. When I put the wrong date in the paper, I encountered the Christian equivalent of a lynch mob, ready to string me up. Our event was Saturday, but the paper announced Sunday. "Look on the bright side," I said with a weak smile. "We'll have lots of visitors for church." No one was amused.

How did I get sucked into these activities in the first place? Simple. Volunteers are a dying breed. Organizations beat the bushes for them, and when they find one, they throw a net of flattery over the unsuspecting prey. "You'd be perfect," they purr.

The poor, foolish person believes them. For awhile. Until she sees a similarity between a toddler with an apple and herself.

Learning to discern between busyness and business is difficult to do. I suspect we must all make our share of mistakes before we can accurately know our capabilities and limitations.

Only in the past two or three years have I been able to accurately assess my abilities and limits. Because I have a strong personality and lots of ideas and enthusiasm, I often am mistaken for a leader. But good leaders are organized and can delegate and follow through. And they have persistence.

I don't. I'm a sprinter, not a distance runner. I don't readily hang in there for the long haul. I lose my enthusiasm and schlep through my job, biding my time, waiting for the end. Short projects work best for me.

Since learning this, it's easier for me to turn down flattering offers for long-term offices. I am better at spearheading committees or simply brainstorming.

Since I have limited time to spend on causes beyond my home and church, I'm learning to consider my strengths when needs and opportunities waltz by. Before getting bamboozled into anything, I ask myself, *Does this use my greatest skills? If not, does God want to build this skill in me? Or is someone better qualified to do it?*

I'm facing a new school year, but I've already decided those volunteer hunters will never take me alive. The middle school PTO needed a treasurer. "Who would like to do this?" the president pleaded.

The principal said, "I hear Mrs. Rabe is good with money."

He's talking about the woman who tried to balance the family checkbook once and put the family a thousand dollars in the hole. No. Mrs. Rabe is not good with money. Mrs. Rabe will not hold a PTO office next year. Nor will she be at the health room. And she probably won't even direct publicity for the school carnival.

That does not mean I won't do anything. But I will do less. I'll use my particular talents where I really am needed—not where I'd like to think I'm needed.

Ecclesiastes 3:1 says there is a season for everything. I've finally realized that seasons follow one another. They don't come simultaneously. My mother says we do different things at different times in our lives. I used to outwardly agree with this, but secretly thought I could be different. Now I know I can't.

Over the years I've also learned that not every season is a time of frantic activity. Fall is a season of winding down, and winter is one of quiet and rest, of death before resurrection. Plants and trees take a snooze and gather strength for the coming spring.

We all need a season of rest to renew our strength. We need time to hibernate, to let our bodies gather new strength for the work ahead. The body that never pauses, stops. Forever.

Rest is wonderful. In fact, it's so beneficial that God designed one day a week to simply ensure our rest. At that time, we're to follow the example of the one who created us (Genesis 2:2). As we follow His example and turn our thoughts toward Him, we renew ourselves for the next season of activity.

Too many times in the past my day of rest was busier than the other six. In addition to all the church activities and undone Saturday chores loomed SUNDAY DINNER, a ritual invented for all the Marthas of the world. Sunday dinner was always impressive and often involved company.

Maybe that's why Sunday dinner was impressive. The family doesn't need impressing. But company. . . !

Entertaining, for many of us, can be an ego thing. We want to fascinate our friends with our culinary skills, our lovely table setting, our general creativeness. So we cook, bake, scrub and clean ourselves into exhaustion—for a few "oohs" and "aahs."

Sometimes we knock ourselves out because of worry born of a lack of self-esteem. If I don't produce an outstanding meal, my friends will be disappointed. They'll think we don't consider them important. They'll scorn my cooking. They'll never come back. I fret.

It doesn't work that way. When was the last time you scorned something someone else cooked? I've discovered most people will happily eat anything they don't have to prepare. They appreciate any effort to give the chef a day off. Besides, our friends don't come to our homes for a free meal. They come to see us, to laugh, to be encouraged. They come for fellowship, not fancy food.

Now our Sunday dinner is easy—hot dogs, hamburgers, soup and bread. If we entertain, the fare is still simple. Sometimes we potluck with friends, everyone contributing so no one must do much. Rest, I am learning, is wonderful.

One family I know gives its mom a day of rest by preparing the meal once a week. Mom can relax while Dad and the boys prepare Sunday dinner. Imagine that—Mother's Day every week!

Even an entire day of rest isn't enough when the other six are packed with feverish activity. No one can "do it all."

Ignore newspaper and magazine articles about spectacular overachievers. Those tales highlight the achievements of a person—the area the individual has poured precious time, talent and energy into. The articles usually don't mention the unfinished chores, neglected talents, lost "opportunites" for service, sacrifices or damaged health. And they certainly don't highlight the failures, broken families or poor relationships with children.

I wish they did. Maybe then we would see that a runner can't win a footrace by trying to jump broad jumps at the same time. He can't get the breath he needs to run if he's singing the national anthem while trotting around the track.

One goal at a time is enough for anyone. The myth of the superwoman who balances family, brilliant career and community service is dead. Many of us need to stop trying to give the poor creature CPR.

I can't afford to go to a health resort for three weeks, so I've decided to become less important. My calendar will have days with nothing written on them. I'll avoid the net of flattery and use my few talents where they're most needed. Instead of covering every base I'll play one position well and let God find team members for the other positions. I'll stand still long enough for my children to see me and know me.

No more rushing from box to box, shuffling apples. I want to make applesauce—not a mess.

Chapter 3

Learning about Leftovers

Leftovers night. Mouths "turned down at the corners" as I slopped various colored dollops onto plates. (The texture didn't vary from one colored dollop to another—it was all like mush.)

"What is this?" Dad asked.

As I identified the mounds, everyone stared as if they could hardly believe their eyes. Warmed scalloped potatoes, now slightly gray, made their third appearance of the week, along with canned creamed corn. A jello salad once topped by a crunchy pretzel crust now sat with all the crunch of fresh worms. These delights were topped by a tossed salad of limp lettuce, squishy tomatoes and dried carrots. Yum.

"Waste not, want not," I chirped. No one smiled. I changed my tactics. "Children in Ethiopia would sell their mothers for a meal like this," I said.

I don't need to relate the reply to that. Most mothers have heard it.

"All right, so it's not Julia Child cuisine. It's food. And it's all you're going to get." I sat down and said grace. (None of the ingrates at the table wanted to perform this service, not even Dad.) I transported a forkful of gray potatoes to my mouth. "Not bad," I mumbled, and thought, *Yuck!*

After dinner, as I scraped leftovers into the garbage, I had a revelation. Do I tend to serve my heavenly Father leftovers too? Do I try the same tricks on Him that I use on my family?

Here it is, God, leftover time. It's all Yours. Wasn't that good of me? I got home from the mall earlier than I expected. Now I can share a few moments with You before the kids get home. . . . Let's see. I've paid Mastercard, Visa, Discover. I've paid the utilities, bought groceries, cat food, new shoes. I need to put aside money for gas and lunch out with friends next week. Since some money is left, I'll write a check to the church.

What does God think about my offerings? He's probably about as enthusiastic about them as He was about Cain's notorious gift. Genesis 4:5 tells us He shoved it aside and said, "Yuck."

I used to read about Cain's rejected offering and wonder if God properly understood the poor guy. After all, Cain wasn't a shepherd. He was a gardener. Fruit and veggies were all he had. What else could he bring to God?

Cain's offering was not an appropriate sin offering. A sin offering required the spilling of blood. Blood both represented the life Adam so faithlessly bartered for a bite of magic fruit and was symbolic of God's provision for our forgiveness through Christ. The real problem wasn't the gift. It was the giver.

Cain had an attitude problem. He was selfish, proud and had no reverence for God. He was the original "rebel without a cause," preferring his own inclinations rather than God's rules. Cain probably spent hours pursuing his interests, but when doing things for God, he was into shortcuts and gave casually. Cain—not God—was master of his life, and his offering reflected that.

Brother Abel, whose offering was accepted, chose and gave the best of his flock—the first-born. He took the first profits from his animal husbandry and forfeited the pleasure of eating it. Instead, he presented it as a gift of love to God. Because he denied himself, the gift meant something. This sacrifice was a symbol of Abel's love as well as a reflection of God's greater love and of the ultimate sacrifice to come through God's Son.

Abel's offering showed the attitude Christ talked about in Mark 12:33. His sacrifice was accepted because it showed what was in his heart. No wonder God was pleased.

Cain, on the other hand, looked around his garden patch and probably reserved the juiciest pomegranates and grapes for himself. He probably brought the next best fruits to the altar in a clay pot, saying, "Here, Father. Look at this good stuff. Eat. Enjoy."

God looked at Cain's casual offering and said, "No way."

According to Mark 12:33, to love God whole-heartedly is better than any other gift. That's the real reason Cain's sacrifice was unacceptable. And that's the real reason why much of what I dish up for God is equally unacceptable. Gifts given out of necessity and half-heartedly are not gifts at all— they're bribes.

What I give of both my time and my posses-sions shows where my heavenly Father is on my priority list. I'm amazed how little I really give Him—especially of my time.

I put in extra hours without blinking if I'm try-ing to make a writing deadline. I wouldn't dream of missing my children's performances or ball-games. I make time for my husband, my friends, my mother.

But do I show that same commitment when God asks for my time? "An extra choir rehearsal this week? I don't know. . . . And I'm not sure I want to sign up to feed visiting missionaries a meal. It's so much extra work . . . . "

Yes, it is extra work, but if my editor asked me to put in some overtime, I wouldn't hesitate be-cause money is involved.

Money is not lasting (it can't even last from one paycheck to the next!), so why would I give it more time than I do God? My friends will fail me. Do they deserve more attention than my heavenly Father? My children will grow up and leave me to lead their own lives. Will the Lord ever leave me?

Of course not. So why would I invest more time in these things than I do in God? A businessperson would say that's a poor investment.

I can see I've mixed my priorities. But how can I actually practice what I've mentally decided?

First, I write my daily devotions at the top of my list of things to do, put my church commitments onto my calendar at the beginning of the month. I can make a special note of holidays, such as Easter and Christmas, and set aside a day in that holiday month to help a worthy Christian cause. Nursing homes are delighted when people bring goodies, and they always look for performing groups or even for someone to play the piano. Food banks need extra food, the missions need donations and workers. I have plenty of options to consider.

Since at church I usually know about special events long before they happen, I can make commitments to these events and plan my other activities accordingly. I can also keep extra food in the freezer for those times when someone at church has a health crisis and needs a prepared meal.

The bottom line is: If I can schedule business meetings and leisure and family activities into my calendar, I can also schedule priority time for serving God.

We've all heard, "You can always find time to do the things you want to do." If God fits in my priorities below my employer, my family and friends and my leisure activities, what does that say about what I really want to do?

The adage "time is money" is right. In fact,

time is worth even more than money. We can always earn more money when we've spent it. But after our time is gone, it's irreplacable.

I guess, Father, whether it's money or time I'm dishing, I show who's most important by who I serve first. Maybe I can get by giving leftovers to my family, but I don't want to present them to You.

SOCIAL
INTERACTION

Chapter 4

Curse God and Die

Everything seemed so easy when we first decided to turn a summer cabin into a permanent residence and live happily ever after without house payments. With no money worries, we'd be able to send my husband back to school for his doctorate degree.

But like many best laid plans of mice and men, this one went awry. Months after the move we still had not achieved financial Utopia. We had passed our budget on the addition and had barely enough money to finish the shell, let alone wire it, plumb it, add sheetrock, paint, carpet, etc.

I was not a happy camper when the five of us moved into our 600-square-foot castle during the June monsoons, but it got worse. . . .

November 13, 1989
Dear Diary:
Since June, I have been sleeping on an army cot in a living room the size of an Afri-

can hut. My kids still don't have doors on
their bedrooms. Certain important words,
like "romance" and "privacy" have dropped
from my vocabulary. The builders have cut
into our roof to add on the new structure
and the roofers are expected next week. Until then, the builders can't make this ark
water tight. The water is dripping from the
ceiling and trickling down the walls. It's
been raining for thirty-nine days and nights.

As we slogged around this afternoon, res-
cuing warped siding and bringing it inside
what will someday be a living room, I suffered a terrible realization—it will be a long
time before I'm out of that army cot. We're
doing the finishing work ourselves as we get
the money! Now that my husband has lost
his job, I know I'll be ready for a nursing
home before my house is ready for me. I
want to run away.

What have I let my husband do to me?
Why has God brought us into this soggy
wilderness? Is this the proper reward for a
woman of God?

During our great outdoors adventure with
the siding, I tripped over a stump and
landed in the mud.

"Are you all right?" asked Hubby Dear. I
had only one thing to say to him, which he
can find in Job 2:9.

* * *

At times, those we love place us in uncomfortable circumstances and we wonder, *What would it be like if this person wasn't in my life, making me miserable?* For every Job's wife who has ever muttered, "Curse God and die. . . . or at least leave," I have these words of hard-learned, profound wisdom: If it isn't Job driving you nuts, it will be Eliphez, Bildad, Zophar, Sam, Harry, Suzie or Mom.

The trouble with this world is it's peopled with people. You run into them everywhere you go. And most of us must either work with or live with them.

Yes, I blamed my husband for my misery, much like my daughter had blamed me for hers weeks before when her disobedience prompted me to put her on restriction. "I hate you!" she had cried.

Hate me? I'd fumed. *Ungrateful child. I'm your mother. I love you. Do you think I like seeing you unhappy? Do you think I lie awake nights dreaming up new ways to torture you?*

I couldn't reason with my daughter. She was determined to blame me for her troubles. But she had contributed to her misery. Her rebellious actions had caused her discomfort.

Reluctantly, I saw the correlation. It was unfair to blame my husband for my present condition when my actions had contributed to the decision and resulting problems. I had agreed to move, thus helping create my current misery. And if we had not devised that particular misery one of us would have found another.

When we go through hard times, why are we comforted by finding someone else to blame? Adam blamed Eve in the garden. Eve blamed the serpent. My daughter blamed me. Job's wife blamed him. I blamed my husband.

Maybe it's a matter of cause and effect. We're taught to find the cause of our suffering, reasoning that if we can correct the cause, we will be rid of our troubles. When we're sick we go to the doctor, learn what's making us ill and get antibiotics to solve the problem. And we often think the rest of life works the same way.

"A rotten job is at the root of my misery. I'll quit and get a new one."

"My misery is caused by another person. I'll get that person out of my life or at least wish him gone."

But solving our personal affairs is usually not so simple because more than one person usually contributes to our suffering. Often one of the people is that hard to blame individual, "me."

Sometimes my children have wished they had anyone but me for a mother. Several times I commanded them to open their eyes and look at the real cause of their troubles. "It's not always someone else's fault! Quit blaming others and admit who really got you into this mess," said the same woman who two years later went bankrupt building a house and became blind herself.

Job's wife blamed her troubles on her husband's insistence on God's goodness. I blamed mine on my husband's search for a better life. Both of us wives came to the same conclusion: "My man is making me miserable. I want to return to the good old days when we didn't have these problems. Why doesn't he just forget going forward, forget doing the right or best thing. Let's just go backward to a comfortable life." (Of course one woman who thought like that is now a pillar of salt somewhere near the Dead Sea.)

Job's wife couldn't see God's hand protecting her husband despite his suffering. Nor could she imagine a happy ending to their story. Maybe she could have retained her patience if she'd known God would reward her husband for his faith and that new days would be even better than the good old days. But maybe God hoped she'd exercise some faith based on His past goodness to them and trust Him even if she couldn't see the future.

God's people don't suffer forever. David eventually earned his kingdom, Joseph was given a high government position, Abraham Lincoln moved from a log cabin to the White House, Corrie Ten Boom survived a Nazi prison camp to become a world evangelist. And our Lord, who endured the ultimate suffering, has now received the ultimate reward.

What kind of fool did Job's wife look like when her husband's trials ended and God vindicated him? What reward did she receive?

Abraham's wife, Sarah, endured much. During his spiritual growing years, Abraham wasn't a heroic lover. Because of his cowardice, Sarah landed in a harem. However, we never see her exclusively blaming her husband for her troubles. Maybe that's why, unlike Job's wife, Sarah doesn't vanish into obscurity. Abraham loved and respected Sarah. He mourned her death and purchased her burial property in the land God had promised them.

Living under the same roof with another flawed human being is the best place to learn love First Corinthians 13 style. We only really start to learn about the high cost of forgiveness or about God's restoring power when another human at the wheel of free choice crashes into unpleasant circumstances and bangs up our lives. And we can't really practice unselfishness until our desires are thwarted. Being kind and giving is easy when no real demands are placed on us. Unselfishness only appears when we're asked to set aside our wants and desires for someone else's. As much as I hate to admit it, I know I don't grow unless I'm stretched. And I don't get strong unless I spend some time hanging on when situations are difficult.

In real life I can't peek to the happy ending of the story like I can when I read a novel, but that's what faith is all about. Ruth and Naomi couldn't see beyond their troubles. Neither could Sarah. But they hung in there.

Maybe, whispered my heavenly Father's familiar voice, *if you complained a little less you'd find your happy ending a little sooner. At least you'd be doing your part to make the interim more pleasant.*

"A gentle answer turns away wrath, but a harsh word stirs up anger" (Proverb 15:1). What was the sense in bullying and berating my husband? Could that stop the rains or make time move faster? It certainly couldn't make our life together very pleasant.

I sighed. "All right, I'll try," I promised.

* * *

After several months on an army cot I began to hope. The framing was done, the addition had electricity and the plumber was coming at the end of the week.

"I think the worst is over," I wrote in my journal. "I hope the worst is over. But if the worst isn't over, help me, Father, to cope. When hard times hit, help me see with eternal eyes. Give me Your perspective. Help me not to make small things big and big things gigantic. Help me see beyond hard circumstances to Your face, nodding, encouraging me. Help me remember that everything in Your universe is moving, including time. Not even the hardest times can remain forever.

"Most of all, help me remember that a wife is a gift from God to a man. I want to be a gift, not a booby prize. Let me remember to be an encourager and a helpmeet, not a hindrance.

"Don't let me forget that my husband and I are a team and that we must work together and encourage each other. Remind me of Honey's high school volleyball team: When one player errs, the others rush to encourage her. 'Shake it off,' they say, then return to their positions, ready to battle for a new point. Help me, Father, to tell my husband when he errs, 'Shake it off. Let's move forward,' not, 'Look what you've done now!'

"Please help me think before I act like Job's wife and say something stupid."

* * *

My house finally was finished. After missing out on getting his doctorate and being laid off for a year, my husband, Job the Second, finished the inside of the house and found a job, taking the family from emotional rapids into calm waters. I now have my own bed and a loving husband to share it with me, as well as a bedroom complete with door and lock. Do I appreciate this bed after all the hard times? You bet! And do those hard times seem so bad in retrospect? Nah!

Too bad I couldn't have been a little less like Job's wife and hung on, waiting for that happy ending. Too bad I couldn't have encouraged instead of nagging. Knowing how life is, I'm sure I'll get another chance to review this lesson.

P.S. I did get another chance. We added onto our house in yet another direction. My husband's company was swallowed by a larger company, eliminating his job. Some lessons apparently need reviewing! So, if you, like me, feel you've failed the first time, don't worry. Our heavenly Father will probably give you another chance to make up the course.

Chapter 5

I'm Not Speaking to You

Twelve-year-old Honey and her best friend weren't speaking. Of course, the argument had been over something incredibly petty—who would serve punch to little kids after church. Each girl felt it was her duty alone. Honey won the honors and her friend did what any other twelve-year-old would do: She gave Honey the silent treatment.

I finally commanded my daughter to go and make up. Honey tried several times but claimed every attempt was met with the words, "I'm not speaking to you."

How childish, I thought. *How ridiculous. How immature!* I didn't know this episode would haunt me a few months later. . . .

We were doing the Sunday morning dash when I said something obnoxious and my husband snarled at me. I could have apologized and eliminated the monster we had just created. But I didn't want to say I was sorry. It wasn't my fault! I clamped my lips and kept them together all the way to church.

I checked my new wound frequently during the service, poking at it and picking the scab. The more I messed with it the uglier and more painful it grew. *My husband truly is a beast! I'm tired of having to worry about every little thing I say. I want him out of my house.*

No! I thought with a sudden burst of nobility. *He loves this house we've worked so hard to build. I'll leave. I'll find some little place and fix it up.*

My mind envisioned a nice condominium with cream-colored carpets, elegantly furnished. And clean, always clean. No jam on the kitchen floor, no dirt ground into the rug, no noise, no cartoons . . .

Naturally, as Hubby would keep the house, he would also have the children. Well, on second thought, I'd take the kids. But he could have them on weekends!

Of course, this was all ridiculous, but I was throwing a mental tantrum. Like a pubescent girl, I wrapped myself in a tattered cloak of injured pride and ignored my mate, refusing to make amends, making myself extremely miserable and loving every minute of it.

Seeing myself as a martyr made me feel important. *Yes, you poor woman, you're so longsuffering. Look at what you endure from this beast.*

A memory tiptoed into my mind of how a relative had not spoken to me for years because of an inconsiderate thing I had said when we were young. Though I had begged his forgiveness, he continued to avoid me or treat me coldly.

Of course, he enjoyed the feeling of power that came with inflicting pain on me, but at what cost? A friendship, personal growth and maturity, good times?

"I've forgiven you," he had claimed. "I just don't want anything to do with you." When he said that I knew I still wasn't forgiven.

And now I was doing the same thing with my husband. "I'm not speaking to you!" The words of Honey's friend echoed in my mind with a sudden flash of insight. I didn't have a clue as to how to practice true forgiveness.

True forgiveness, I realized, must reflect God's forgiveness. God will always wipe the slate clean and start again (2 Chronicles 7:14; Psalm 103:12; 1 John 1:9). Time after time the Father put behind him the idolatry and faithlessness of His first chosen people, Israel. He'd start over with them when they repented, treating them as if they'd never sinned.

And His forgiveness encompasses more than that nation. It extends to all of His creation. Any who wish to be forgiven their ignorance and rebelliousness may come to the Father and find a fresh start. All who are sorry may be treated as if they'd never strayed.

God's forgiveness involves deliberate forgetfulness. If our forgiveness truly reflects His love, should we focus on hurts dished to us or should we behave as if the wrong never occured? Surely anything less is not true forgiveness.

When carried around and frequently remembered, the vision of old hurts becomes distorted. We look at the person who hurt us and can only see the ugly and the unlikeable. In a sense of self-protection we keep our distance. As a result, neither person changes. The relationship remains stagnant and poisoned. In short, nothing about us is any different from the rest of the world. We hold grudges, we avoid, we may even verbally shoot our enemy in the back ("Do you want to know why I won't come to your house if Suzie is going to be there? Well, I'll tell you . . ."). In these situations, we have no new start, no rebuilding, no new growth, no change—and no witness.

I realized I needed to treat someone who has wounded me as if the painful words never left his mouth. But how could I start? Offering a plate of cookies, perhaps? Making a phone call just to say hi? Even if his treatment left my emotions begrudging, I had to begin the actions of forgiveness. How about a basic "Have a Nice Day" card? Could I, perhaps, throw some business this person's way? Even if the person refused to spend time with me, though forgiveness doesn't mean forcing myself on anyone, it does mean not needing to keep remembering how I've been hurt. I need to let go of such hurts. And if I happen to encounter such a person, my responsibility is to offer a kind greeting, not sarcasm or coldness.

Then there was my husband . . . oh yes, him.

My husband apologized after church and the vision of the quiet, sparsely but elegantly furnished condo evaporated. *But what*, asked my heavenly Father, *would have happened if you had let your anger continue building such a small thing to Goliath proportions?*

I squirmed. If we had continued the cold war through the day and into the next, what would have happened? Is that how a couple builds incompatability? One grudge at a time? It would certainly be easy to lay our hurts like bricks, making a foundation on which to build resentment.

How quickly the good things can be covered and forgotten. How quickly our anger can transport us from a bad situation to a worse development. That must be why Ephesians 4:26 tells us not to end the day if we're still angry with someone. Today's wounds harden overnight into tomorrow's grudges.

And grudges simply aren't an option for Christians.

Jesus told his followers in Matthew 6:14-15 that if they couldn't forgive those who hurt them they shouldn't expect God to forgive them. Those words seemed harsh, but that's how seriously the Father takes the sin of unforgiveness.

We can remove ourselves from dangerous circumstances, but God does not command us to harbor resentment or try to punish those who've damaged us. Deuteronomy 32:35-36 tells us that punishment is God's business. Trying to get even is a waste of time and spiritual energy. It also distracts us from the more important issue of growing and looking to the future.

Many squabbles down the road from my first lesson, I still must work hard to capture my runaway imagination before it turns small offenses into capital ones.

If I let the unrighteous anger of selfishness control my thoughts I'll only see how I was wronged. I'll only find ideas for how to hurt back. This whole process is not productive and should be stopped as soon as it starts.

Who gets to pour the punch? Who gets the last word? Who gets the recognition? Who cares? I'm learning that regarding those wounds we all occasionally inflict on each other, our most important question is not "Who caused this wound to the relationship?" but "Who will be the first to bind it?"

Chapter 6

The End of the World

"**B**ut you promised," Junior tearfully murmured as we tucked him in bed. "I'm sorry you didn't get to watch *The Glob That Ate New York Meets the Teenage Mutant Ninja Slugs*. But tomorrow is Friday and you can stay up late to watch it then," I promised.

The thundercloud didn't lift from Junior's face.

"I'm sorry we ran out of time," added Dad. "We'll do better tomorrow."

"But you said I could watch it tonight," Junior insisted.

"I know, and I'm sorry that didn't work out," said Dad.

"But," began Junior.

"Tomorrow," I said and shut the door on my guilt-inflicting son.

All right. We'd goofed. We'd promised and failed to deliver. Junior hadn't been able to watch the inane movie he'd seen six times before. He had asked at dinner if he could watch his favorite video and we had given him the casual "yes" parents often utter without thinking. Then we'd worked on an assortment of projects and the movie had been forgotten—until I said, "Time to get ready for bed."

Anyway, we would make it up to Junior the next night. This wasn't the end of the world or economic collapse. Why couldn't Junior understand that?

OK, I know the obvious answer to that. He was a child. And what may seem unimportant to adults is often vital to a child. But more was involved than that.

All this "you promised" stuff really boiled down to one thing: Junior wanted his way, and when he didn't get it, he was unhappy.

Junior, I must admit, is determined. Whether it's a particular after-school snack or permission to have company, he likes to get what he wants. And when he doesn't get it, he doesn't give in graciously. Instead he turns into King of the Beasts. (Behavior which usually results in his being caged in his room!)

I could still hear Junior howling in his bedroom. *How immature,* I thought. *How childish!*

Does this remind you of anyone we know? whispered my heavenly Father.

"Certainly not," I replied huffily. "I'm a mature adult."

I could almost see my Father's expression, the same loving, gently mocking one I gave my children. *Really?*

"All right," I admitted. "I like to get my way a little."

A little?

"A lot."

Why?

Good question. Why, indeed? Let's start with the obvious. Sometimes I just want my way because I want my way. I'm just thinking of me, and that's who I want to please. That's pretty straightforward, ugly and easy to deal with. Sometimes the underlying motivation is more complex. Like when I want my way because I feel others' respect or love hinges on my behavior. I worry what will happen if I can't meet those expectations.

I still remember an incident from the early days of my marriage revolving around basketball. My oldest nephew played high school basketball and had a big game one night. All the family would be there. I planned to go too. All good aunts attended their nephews' big games and cheered them to victory (or, in my family's case, hollered, coached the coach and embarrassed the star player).

My husband was not a good aunt. He felt we'd spent enough time with my family and wanted to attend a college game at his alma mater.

I didn't give in graciously. I wept. Copiously. We were at dinner with my in-laws, and I'm sure they wondered what kind of woman their son had married. "Why all this fuss over a basketball game? Why is she insisting on getting her way?"

Why, indeed? Because I wanted to be a good aunt. I wanted to be supportive. I wanted to do what I felt was expected. I wanted my way, and if I didn't get it I was sure my family would never speak to me again.

I didn't get my way. And I wasn't very happy about it. But I survived. My nephew also survived. So did the rest of my family. No one stopped speaking to me. Since that incident I've missed many other important family events, but none stopped because of my absence.

I still like to get my way when it involves pleasing others—from working with the music for church services or entertaining houseguests to serving on a committee. The problem comes when my activities crowd into the lives of my other family members. Schedules conflict. Who will be away and doing? Who will rearrange a schedule or not do at all? Who will get his or her way? Who won't? "But people depend on me," I say.

"People depend on me too," says my husband.

"They depend on me more," I insist. I want my way! I need my way. I simply must sing for the next sixty worship services. If I can't, everyone will be mad. God will never use me again, the service will fail. . . .

Get real, Sheila. Quit thinking you are so important that the world hinges on whether or not you get your way.

I wonder if I sometimes want my way because pride has gotten tangled up in my plans. When my projects go well and enthusiastic flatterers gush, "Was this your idea?" or "Did you do all this work?" it's always nice to answer, "Why, yes."

Sometimes I want my way because I honestly feel it's better. My way will be more fun. My way will look nicer or be more efficient.

And wanting my way isn't always wrong. When I'm morally right I want to stand firm.

"Yes, I want 'my way.' I want to see pornography stamped out, not because I want to tell others what they can do, but because I believe it adversely affects this society. My children are potential victims. For my children's safety and future I'll fight to get 'my way.'" "No, daughter. You can't go out with that cute non-believer. I insist on my way because it's best for you."

It's important to fight to get our own way when a child's self-worth or spiritual development is involved. "I know you're tired, dear, but we need to attend Junior's Sunday school program. He'll be disappointed if we don't. And he'll question the worth of church involvement if his parents don't show support."

Sometimes, even on important matters, when I'm sure I'm morally or practically right, I still don't get my way. Sometimes I have to say my piece, do what I think I should, and if I'm ineffective, say, "OK, Father. I tried. You handle it from here."

Many years ago, our church considered enlarging and redecorating the sanctuary and foyer and adding to the fellowship hall. The church leaders told the congregation they wanted to be sure this plan was God's will, so they would collect pledges. If they could do this project without incurring debt they would go ahead. Though pledges fell short, the leaders decided, "We'll proceed. But we'll have to take a loan."

Mine was one of the voices raised in protest. "What happened to God's will?" I demanded. "This is crazy. You can't say one thing and do another."

No one listened and I felt like a prophetess without honor in her own land.

But contrary to my fears, everything worked out fine, and I enjoyed the benefits of the project as much as anyone. Today the loan is long paid off.

God is a lover of diversity. You can find as many colors to paint a kitchen as you find in a rainbow or a moutain meadow. Each one is lovely. Each color appeals to a different person, but no one color is better than another. You can choose one of an endless variety of themes for a women's luncheon. My ideas may be good. So might someone else's.

My way is not the only way to spend time or money, decorate a house or even worship on Sunday morning. So maybe if someone else with a different opinion is as strongly in favor of his or her opinions as I am mine, I could give in.

Does this include letting my sixteen-year-old daughter wear a baseball cap backward on her head? Sigh. It probably does.

Right now my husband and I are disputing over how to finish a balcony off of our bedroom. My way is better. I am certain. My husband has thanked me for my input, but plans to do the job his own way. If it turns out badly I'll experience some irritation and inconvenience. But really, I wonder, is this worth squabbling over? In the eternal scheme of life, does it really matter? Probably no more than my son waiting a day to watch his video.

Sometimes, like my son, I want my way because it means pleasure for me. If that pleasure is denied or threatened, I can get ugly. When Junior was young, he could cry crocodile tears, but his mom could cry elephant ones. However, as my young son showed me, that is hardly a mature reaction. Scheming, wheedling and whining aren't good either.

What can I do when nobody else wants to go my way? Sometimes, I'm learning, I can soothe the irritation by playing "It's better than . . ." If I want Chinese food but everyone else wants Mexican, I can remind myself it's better than not going out at all. I want more money in our checking account; my husband wants to save for retirement. So I have less money to spend than I want. At least I have some money. Sleeping on an army cot is better than sleeping in my car or on the street. Having a small budget for groceries is better than having no money for food.

I guess this is what Paul was talking about in Philippians 4:11: "For I have learned to be content whatever the circumstances."

Besides playing "It's better than . . . " I can also console myself with promises of "another time" or compromise between my way and someone else's. I can't always talk my husband into a massive party for dozens of people, but I can usually talk him into hosting another couple or family. An expensive vacation may be out, but a trip to see friends nearby is possible.

Frank Sinatra extolled the virtue of a person living his or her life in the song "My Way." Sometimes I still hear that song on the radio. The music is beautiful, but when I really listen to the lyrics I decide the hero of the song was rather a brat.

"Father, am I rather a brat at times?" I ask.

At times, answers my Father honestly. *But I still love you.*

Just like I love my son. "Thanks, Father," I say and try not to look at the balcony.

SOCIAL INTERACTION, ADVANCED COURSE

Chapter 7

That's So Dumb!

"I'm so sure, Honey. What do you know?" Junior challenged his sister.

"Junior. I've been on this earth three years longer than you. I think I know a little more than you do," Honey snapped back.

"At least *I'm* doing good in school."

"At least *I* don't chew with my mouth open."

"Enough!" I commanded. "If you can't say something nice don't say anything at all."

Too bad I never realized I needed to take that advice myself. Until . . .

During Operation Desert Storm, the television stayed on, providing constant news updates for all of us who were praying and/or worrying. With my close friend and houseguest, Betty Buddy, I listened to the news and discussed the war.

Like myself, Betty enjoys causes. But the causes we get involved in are usually as unique as our approaches to the same problem. This time was typical. Betty told me about the prayer vigil and peace march she had attended. "We were led in a special prayer," she said. "Then we chanted, 'Peace, give us peace.' "

"Now what good does that do?" I demanded. "The Bible says they'll cry peace, peace, and there is no peace. Surely these people could find a better way to pray."

I continued, giving my unrequested opinions, setting my friend straight. Every time poor Betty tried to defend her actions, I squelched her with my smarter-than-thou put downs.

"Well, we all have different ministries," she said diplomatically.

"Since when is marching around chanting, 'Peace, peace' a ministry?" I snorted.

Betty looked at me and I suddenly understood the meaning of that cliché, "If looks could kill I'd be dead."

Why did my good friend look at me like that? What was wrong with her? What had I said? All right, I knew what I'd said. But was that any reason to glare?

Now I was angry. "Would you rather I never disagreed with you?" I insisted. "Would you rather I never had an opinion?"

Several days later I realized there is a big difference between having an opinion and being opinionated. My friend had an opinion. *I* was opinionated.

"If you can't say something nice don't say anything at all." My words to my children hung before me as if on a giant blackboard.

"Me, Father? You mean me?"

You told your friend she was stupid.

"I never said that!"

You basically said that when you dismissed what she had done. How else was she to interpret your remarks?

I knew the Father was right. My friend was raised in an atmosphere of abuse, never able to please. No matter what she had said or done, it had always been wrong—not good enough. Though I hadn't meant to direct my words at her personally, she'd taken them that way because she was involved in the activity I was attacking.

What was the difference between my children's put-downs and the way I had treated my friend? Nothing.

Why do we put down other people? Maybe we mistakenly believe it builds us up. *You're dumb, therefore I'm smart. You're wrong and I'm right. Your actions are ridiculous because they are different from mine. Let me show you how bad you are so you'll see how good I am. Then you'll want to be like me and do as I do.*

Does this tactic ever work? I don't think so. It never worked on my children. I was never able to shame them into better behavior with a put-down. That only taught them, by example, how to inflict similar misery on each other.

As for my friend, the only opinion she changed after my harangue was her opinion of me. And it didn't change for the better!

"A man convinced against his will is of the same opinion still," goes the old saying. Any sentence that starts with phrases such as "That's so stupid,"

"Anyone with half a brain ought to know" or "How can you believe?" won't accomplish anything because these words are packed with criticism, bound to make people defensive. And a defensive person is as moldable as stone.

Anyway, who was I to try to shove my friend into my mold? Had her actions been wrong or immoral? Hardly. So what did it matter? Why did I have to make such a big deal about it? And, more importantly, did I really have a right to judge whose works were useful and whose weren't? Were my actions any more productive than Betty's?

Only God can truly judge the worth of a work, for only God can see the heart. I can imagine what was in Betty's heart the day she made her peace march. Since I know Betty is a caring person, it was probably something noble. What was in my heart the day I "helped" Betty see the error of her ways? Pride, pure and simple.

I once heard an activist on a television talk show who was so angry and abusive that the entire studio audience turned against him. He excused his actions by announcing that kindness wouldn't accomplish anything. But his behavior didn't bring results either. By harangering his audience he drove away the very people he hoped to win to his cause. People lost sight of his message because of the way it was delivered.

Ephesians 4:2 commands us to have patience with each other. Even when a fellow Christian stumbles, we are to set him or her right, not with an attitude of superiority, but with gentleness and an understanding of our own humanity (Galatians 6:1).

And speaking of correcting . . . a painfully embarrassing image came to mind. It was of myself, offering "input" in the adult Sunday school class. Every Sunday. Several times.

Did you really need to say everything you've said these past few weeks? whispered my Father. *Must you comment on everything you disagree with? Do you really need to add to what the teacher says? Who's teaching this class—you or the teacher?*

Ouch! But how right. If our ultimate goal is to build the Body of Christ and glorify the Father, then building ourselves at others' expense is unacceptable behavior. Not every statement a person makes needs someone to disagree with it. Always being right is not only humanly impossible, it's irritating. And nothing is worse than having someone in your Sunday school class who thinks he or she is always right.

Also, nothing is worse than having a friend who's always right. I take that back—something is worse than having a friend who's always right. That's having a friend who's always right and puts you down to show how right she is. If my words aren't building others, they're probably tearing them down.

"If you can't say anything nice, don't say anything at all." My mother said it and I said it, thinking it applied to kids. I'm realizing it does. It applies to God's kids, young and old.

Chapter 8

"Play Together Nicely"

Once upon a time three mothers got together, each bringing her assorted grade-school progeny. The moms visited while the children played outside. Let me make a correction. The moms tried to visit while the children wandered in and out, each child complaining about the others.

"Play together nicely," said the moms and shooed the children outside, only to have them return.

Now, one of these parents was very wise (or thought she was). She tried to share wisdom with the children. "Why don't you all play a game together, like baseball or soccer or kick the can," she suggested.

But she had cast pearls before swine. The children couldn't agree on what to play, so they played nothing.

"What a waste," the wise mother lamented.

"You could have done all kinds of things if you'd just agreed on something."

Years later, as this quasi-wise mother left a women's prayer meeting, her words haunted her. The group had been praying about a situation and as one woman prayed, Wise Mother thought, *I can't agree with this woman at all. Is she crazy? Well, I just won't pray along on this one.*

As I drove home, I encountered a new understanding of an old revelation. Christ had promised His disciples that if even just two of them asked something in prayer, He would grant their request.

So why do so many prayers seem to go unanswered? I wondered. Could one of the reasons be a lack of cooperation among body members? Do we sometimes hide a lack of unity under a cloak of politeness?

"Good heavens, Father!" I exclaimed. "Surely no correlation lies between mature adults and squabbling children trying to agree on what to play."

Maybe it does, said the Father.

* * *

I thought about myself. How many times had I sat with others, pretending to be a functioning part of a unit, when my mind was wandering a hundred miles away, or maybe only five miles away to my messy house. How many times had I pretended to agree with the person praying when

I didn't agree at all. Prayer meeting would end and I'd go home, thinking that because my body had been present, I had accomplished something for God's kingdom. Really, I had contributed nothing.

Instead of rattling off twenty prayer requests and praying haphazardly, perhaps a good way to run a prayer meeting would be to list needs and examine, "What are we asking? How shall we agree to pray for this?"

If prayer is part of spiritual warfare, shouldn't we take aim? Shouldn't our prayers have power, like a karate expert's kick? All the power of such a person's body is centered in his or her foot upon kicking.

Shouldn't our prayers operate on the same principle: the hearts and strength of many poured into one focused, powerful prayer? Many parts of the Body, but all having the same mind, the mind of Christ?

What about the nitty-gritty stuff of church life? What about the women's ministries, the committees and all those other breeding grounds for disagreement and trouble? I can remember so many small squabbles that arose over little things! Many times I saw women pull away from a group, running to complain to the Father that the others weren't acting the way they expected. "They won't play my way. Make them do it my way or I won't play! I won't come to the women's meetings. Maybe I won't even come to this church any more. That'll show 'em."

I couldn't immediately remember instances in which I'd left the play yard, but I knew at times I'd pulled away emotionally and mentally. And if I was doing that, how many others were also? How much more could we have done if I'd stayed, if we'd all stayed?

The next time this "wise mother" meets with fellow believers, I will bring more than my body. I will behave as a functioning part of the unit, co-operating with others, contributing what I can. I won't be a whining child, mentally leaving the group to complain to the Father about my companions' inadequacies. In short, I'll remember the Father's words, a variation on my own words to a yard full of children, "Pray together nicely."

Chapter 9

Cracking Knees
and Rattling Tongues

Honey stood in the family room cracking her knees.

"Don't do that to your knees," I said for the bezillionth time.

"I don't know how Honey can stand to do that," put in Junior.

"Mr. Perfect," muttered Honey.

Poor Honey. Ever since Junior got old enough to say "sibling rivalry," he has found ways to put her down or to get her in trouble to make himself look good by comparison. "Mom! Honey just . . ." "Why does Honey always . . . ?" "Mom, do you think it's right that Honey . . . ?"

Junior never tells me when Honey's done something good. But when he has dirt to dish out, he comes running, tattling with an angel's face to cover his devilish motives.

This for the sister who sounded the alarm when

her baby brother accidentally dropped his teddy bear out the car window. Honey's insistence made me stop the car and risk certain death to rescue the hopelessly grungy, well-loved toy.

And this from the boy who once, thinking I had forgotten his sister and was about to drive off without her, cried in panic, "Honey!"

Of course, Honey has tattled in her time too. And always with the same self-righteous air as her brother.

How can these children be so loyal to each other one moment and become backstabbers the next? I mused. Why would they want to do such a thing to each other?

Why, indeed? prompted a familiar small voice. *Think about your own behavior. Perhaps the answer lies there.*

My *behavior? I don't act like that!* I insisted.

Oh?

I tried to feign ignorance, but it was hard to pretend I'd forgotten a recent phone conversation with my friend, Flicka, when I did my own tattling.

Still smarting from an earlier disagreement with our mutual pal, Minnie, I waited for just the right moment to introduce the subject burning on my tongue. At last I had my chance. "Minnie must be under a lot of stress," I observed innocently. Then I related the rude, immature thing Minnie had said to me the day before.

For a moment I felt better. I'd showed Flicka how flawed Minnie was. Flicka would see how I'd been mistreated. She'd agree that Minnie's behavior had been childish. I'd be marked for sainthood and Minnie would be seen as the selfish beast she truly was. So there!

Of course, the only problem was that Minnie isn't any more selfish than I am. And I am no less flawed than she is.

My plan backfired. Flicka didn't commiserate or even press me for more details. (See if I call her again!) I felt like a rat for my self-righteous tattling, which was nothing more than selfishness in disguise.

This brought me back full circle to Junior and Honey. I felt like I'd made a real discovery. That's why they tattle—the bottom line is selfishness! Hmmm. In kids you expect to deal with that sort of thing. In adults . . . aren't we supposed to be beyond that?

Many of us would say we are. That's because we don't call tattling by its real name. We call it gossip, as in gossip columns, which are just supposed to be fun and entertaining; as in telling a good story; as in "I'm sure Suzie won't mind." (Won't she? Did you ask Suzie if you could tell on her?)

Jody Berg, a young woman who recently joined our church family, has a gift for recognizing gossip and saying, "I don't need to know that about her" whenever someone starts to spin out a good story.

I've learned a lot from Jody. I'm starting to understand that what we hear about people becomes like tinted windows, coloring the way we see them. If we verbally tint someone in a bad light, we put dark glasses on their fellow Christians.

That individual can have done zillions of great things for God, but the dark glasses we've passed out will blind others to the good and enlarge the ugly.

As Christians, we prefer not to use the word "gossip," because it has bad connotations. Instead, we call it "sharing" or "concern." We come together with angelic faces and devilish motives. Then we put our friends and fellow Christians under a gigantic microscope and magnify their flaws. All this so we can make ourselves feel or look better by comparison. It's the old speck versus the mote issue.

We hate it when our kids tattle, even though it starts quite naturally and understandably. When my children were little, I expected them to run to me to settle their disputes. I was the judge and author of justice in their kingdom. To whom else could they go? They didn't yet have the skills to settle their own differences.

Now they're older and tattling is no longer necessary, so like all good mothers, I discourage it.

Somehow, when adults are involved, it's harder to discourage. But maybe if we want to break the habit among ourselves, we should do what we do when our children come to us to tattle.

When one of my little darlings tattles, I do one of two things. I cut him or her off, refuse to listen and send him packing, or I sit both kids down together and make them settle their differences.

I can't always force my friends to sit down and settle their differences. But I can encourage them to talk out their misunderstandings: "What a shame you and Gina had that problem on the tennis court, Sue. Maybe you should call her and straighten things out." This is much better than saying, "Yeah, you're right. Gina was unreasonable." Maybe Gina was unreasonable, but I wasn't there, so how can I know?

Disputes between friends are like those between kids. The complainer is giving only one side of the story—hers. And, with only hearing half of the story, how can I take sides? I could be taking the wrong one.

Anyway, if I did take a side how could I help Gina and Sue make up? The beautitude says the peacemakers will be blessed, not the sidetakers.

So instead of taking sides, I'll encourage my friends to deal with their problems directly, following the advice in Matthew 18. If I'm a listening ear in a dispute, I'd better make sure both friends are present, not just one complainer.

My friend, Flicka, was wise to ignore me, just as I ignore many of my children's accusations. By moving the subject on, she showed me the insignificance of my complaint. Feeling small was not pleasant, and it effectively discouraged me from tattling on Minnie to anyone else.

Not all my friends are as good at nipping my bad behavior in the bud as Flicka. I have a hard time stopping the gossip flow. I'm curious. And besides, gossip is better than TV because I myself know all the characters involved. And I'm always sure I can help them if I have all the pertinent details. And even if I can't, I still like to hear all the dirt, because then I can congratulate myself on how superior I am or remind my fellow gossiper that I predicted that person would have these problems. (Then my friend will congratulate me on my superiority!)

But as Christians, we're all the Body of Christ, and we're to work together, not against each other. We are to build each other, not destroy each other. When the Body of Christ turns against itself, it loses its power to witness. I have to admit my witness has been spoiled more than once by my big mouth.

When my friends can't or won't police me, I must police myself. Before recounting any incident, I'll ask, "Am I tattling? Does this anecdote show another person in a bad light? What are my motives for sharing this?"

James 4:11 and First Timothy 5:13 tell me not to be a gossip. The Amplified version of Leviticus 19:16 cautions me in very strong terms to not go around being a "dispenser of gossip."

The first time I read that verse I thought of soap dispensers. Push on the bar and out comes the soap. Am I a little dispenser? Are you? Does someone just have to push the gossip bar for us to open our mouths and out it comes?

In First Timothy, Paul points to idleness as the breeding ground for gossip. Busy people with important things on their minds may be the subject of gossip, but they generally don't do much of it. They don't have time.

I know when I'm wrapped up in work, I don't have time to chat on the phone or lounge around a friend's kitchen table discussing someone else. My mind is on other things. That's where it needs to be. I've heard that small people talk about other people; great people talk about ideas. I like that, and I think it's true.

I don't need to show my every emotional "ouchie" to everyone who likes the sight of blood. Minor nicks and scratches can heal fine without my running to the nearest friend for attention.

The person I need to run to is the Lord. First Peter 5:7 tells me to give Him my cares. He can give me wisdom to deal with difficult situations and to speak to the heart of whomever I'm having difficulties with. And He won't gossip!

I remember one incident in which I didn't tattle to anyone about another person's flaws. Keeping my opinions to myself, I concentrated on that friend's good points and asked the Father to take care of the situation. And He did! I was so amazed and so proud of myself. And God worked in that person's life without my having to tell anyone about her flaws.

I know each of my children's weak areas, and I don't need a sibling to point them out to me. If I know my children so well, how much better must my heavenly Father know my faults and those of my spiritual siblings.

I think I finally understand that the Father feels the same way I do; He can deal with His children without any help from tattlers.

MOM'S LESSONS IN ECONOMICS

"Economics is a subject for math majors and advisors to the president and people who can balance their checkbook, I protested. I don't understand anything about it."

I know, said the Father. *And I think you'll be so much happier once you do.*

MOM'S ECONOMIC OUTLOOK

Chapter 10

I Scream, You Scream

Baby Dolly wasn't happy. She was starving and I was not shovelling the food into her mouth fast enough. She cried between mouthfuls, as if to say, "Hurry! Can't you see I'm starving?" Her crying made it difficult for me to feed her.

"It's all right. It's coming," I crooned. "Mama won't let you starve. Doesn't Mama always feed you, silly girl? When have you ever gone without?"

* * *

My words to my baby daughter echoed in my mind. I knew who was whispering them to me. And I knew why.

The last few years had been one big struggle, and unlike those heroines in the books who revel in the fight, put their shoulder to the wheel, face the storm with exultation, etc., I hadn't enjoyed myself one bit. Much like my baby I had opened my mouth and cried, even as the Father was spooning in the sustenance I needed.

Dolly didn't need to cry. I wouldn't let her starve. She cried anyway, knowing only her hunger, not yet understanding that her mother would always feed her.

Can you see My caring presence is as real in your life as yours is in your daughter's? whispered the Father.

How true! Yet I seemed to wail every time my stomach or purse needed filling. And I had the patience of my baby.

"All right, Father. I know You have everything I need to survive and grow. I know Your love for me is even greater than mine for my child's. I will trust You."

That's what I said. But the spoon didn't always get to my mouth quickly enough, and when it did it wasn't as full as I wanted it. "Wah!"

"I'm tired of worrying about money," I complained one day.

Then don't, said the Father.

"I beg your pardon?"

You should.

"No. I mean, what did You say?"

I said, *"Don't."* *Don't worry about money. Nobody asked you to do so. I certainly never required it of you. Remember your words to your baby? Has she missed a meal yet?*

"Of course not," I replied, insulted.

Have you?

"No," I admitted.

Why is that?

"Because You're taking care of me?" I guessed.

Your constant lack of faith wounds Me, child. That's what worry is, you know.

Lack of faith. The Father was right. Every time I worried I was basically saying to Him, "You can't take care of me."

As I chewed on this problem, I realized I had to take two steps. First, I had to make myself a spiritual foundation. Second, I had to build on that foundation with practical action.

After reading several Old Testament passages I realized the spiritual foundation was not a new concept. God had done this with His people for a long time, starting with the nation of Israel.

The ritual celebration of the Passover was meant to be a tool of remembrance:

> Remember well what the LORD your God did to Pharaoh and to all Egypt. You saw with your own eyes the great trials, the miraculous signs and wonders, the mighty hand and outstretched arm, with which the LORD your God brought you out. The LORD your God will do the same to all the peoples you now fear. (Deuteronomy 7:18-19)

Think; remember. Regularly remind yourselves of the things I have done for you. This is how you will know you can trust Me—by My past faithfulness.

In Luke 22:19, Jesus gave new symbolism to the Passover. He said that every time we eat this bread and drink this wine we should remember what He has done for us.

We can build a firm foundation for the future by looking at the past and remembering what God has done for us. The psalmist used this tool in several psalms, including: 66, 78, 81, 104 and 105.

All these psalms remind the nation of Israel what God had done for them. God's care for His people is a spiritual law as dependable as any physical law. "Remember how God has always come through for us," says the psalmist. "Let your past experiences be proof of God's faithfulness and trust Him."

Following the example in Scripture, I began to recount instances of God's provision in my own life: the first home He miraculously provided, the bags of groceries we received when the Christian school where my husband taught hit lean times, the odd jobs that came our way when we were desperately low on funds, my first royalty check. We never had great wealth, but just as Jesus promised His disciples in Matthew 6:32-33, we never lacked for what we really needed.

These are my personal psalms, I thought. *I need to recite these when things get scary.*

Becky, our pastor's wife, keeps a scrapbook to remind her of God's faith and goodness. In it she has snapshots and even pictures from magazines to represent God's provision. A picture of a car reminds her family of the time God saved them from a terrible car accident. A picture of a vacation spot with a dollar sign next to it symbolizes an unexpected bounty that provided for a family vacation.

God is faithful, and we can prove it by pointing to His past faithfulness to us. Just as old Newton's apple will always fall down, so will God watch over those who serve Him. It's a proven spritual law.

In addition to my past experiences, I also have God's promises. My favorite verse is Psalm 37:25, "I have been young, and now am old; yet have I not seen the righteous forsaken, nor his seed begging bread" (KJV). I appreciate other verses too: Psalm 28:7; Psalm 31:19; Psalm 32:10; Psalm 34:17-19; Psalm 37:4-5; Matthew 6:25-33; First Peter 5:7. With these verses and the remembrance of God's past provision, I can lay my spiritual foundation. This is the first step to putting my mind at rest. Quoting these verses to myself and recounting experiences are the mental exercises that build my faith muscles and make them strong. And strong faith muscles are all that stand between me and worry.

But God expects me to build on the foundation He's given me. That's where step two enters. Israel had to physically act on God's promises to deliver them by leaving Egypt. When confronted with economic challenges, I must also take action. Practices like budgeting, saving and doing without appear in my textbook, because God expects me to act responsibly, to work to earn my keep and to spend wisely the resources He gives me.

Over the years our money problems were usually the result of unwise spending. While God promised to provide for our needs, I realized He wasn't so indulgent a parent as to always protect us from the results of our greed-inspired stupidity.

When the money was mismanaged we couldn't complain and worry. We needed to act. Sometimes tightening our belts was enough. But at other times, toilet paper and gas for the car became luxury items and like the Proverbs 31 lady, I had to buy a field (or, in current terms, get a job).

I was not fond of working. Let me rephrase that. I enjoyed working—at home. I liked being my own boss in charge of my own day. Between home and church, my hobbies and my friends and my family's activities, I had all the fulfillment I craved. Getting an outside job didn't appeal to me at all.

But getting out of debt did. And rather than have my husband take a second job—which meant the family would never see him—I took a part-time job. Through rough years, I took several part-time jobs and some of them were pretty bizarre.

I did it all, from burping plasticware to singing telegrams. I even had a short-lived career as a kindergarten gymnastics teacher. This ended when I tripped over a practice balance beam ("Who left that on the floor in plain sight, anyway?") and landed on my nose before my class and several stunned parents. As I scrambled, often forgetting step one while doing step two, the Father reminded me that I am not the savior of my family.

And neither is my husband. (We both learned that when he got laid off after fifteen years with the same company, and then again three years later.)

The true provider for our family is our heavenly Father. And to make sure I really got the point, the Father rarely provided for us in the same way twice. When, as a writer, I began turning my morning trip to the mailbox into a pilgrimage, the Father delayed the expected check or, worse yet, let rejection slips greet me instead of acceptances for my articles and short stories. Ah-ah. The mailman is not your provider.

When I was playing in a band, we had a long, dry spell with no bookings. "Your talent alone won't provide for you either," said the Father.

When my husband, the Prudential Rock, got laid off, that was the final examination. And it was a long one, lasting a year. In spite of everything I'd learned, I struggled through it for eleven-and-a-half-months, taking part-time jobs, worrying, whining, crying. "I hate this! The spoon isn't full enough!"

But it was. And we survived.

I've seen God direct other families through similar rough times. My friend Huguette's husband was out of work for over three years. She also experienced a jobless period of time. I asked Huguette what she learned from that experience and she replied, "God is great!" She says God used that hard time to draw her family closer to Him. They naturally prayed for jobs because they wanted to pay their debts, but looking back she realized God had more important needs to meet first—the need to learn to trust Him.

Huguette's family isn't rich now. They don't own their home, even though they once had two. They sold both to pay their debts. But more important, the whole family is happy and doing volunteer work for God in the local church.

Shawn and her family moved from California to Washington and bought a home, hoping their house in California would sell. It didn't and they had to carry two mortgages. Business struggles coupled with an IRS battle brought down the financial roof. The family lost both houses and their savings. For several years they teetered on the edge of ruin.

Reviewing their years of struggle, Shawn says she realizes she and her husband had trusted in all the wrong things. However, hard as their circumstances were, the family never went without a meal. Shawn's husband became a Christian, and she learned to walk closely with God. Now that the family business is prospering and the couple is finding their feet financially, she refers to their struggles as an opportunity rather than a trial. Her new goal is not to collect new material possessions but to remain unattached to those she has.

After studying my own life lessons and those of my friends, I know what I'd write if God were to give me a written exam on this subject: I budget, I work, I try not to be wasteful. And I believe as I put God first in spending both my time and my money, He will honor my commitment. He will keep my family from starving in the streets. He won't necessarily give us great material wealth, but He'll take care of our needs. Circumstances have shaken the finanical house of Rabe. A few windows fell out, some unnecessary decoration fell off, but the house survived because the foundation is built on solid rock: God's faithfulness.

Each time we've struggled with unemployment, Mom, the big baby, has cried for food, even though her heavenly Father had prepared it already.

I'm here, said the Father. *Open your mouth, not to cry, but to let Me feed you. It's so much easier when you're not crying.*

The Father is right. Eating is a lot easier when you're not crying. And the food tastes better too!

Chapter 11

Sinking Boats
and Falling Sparrows

S teamboat Lake, Eastern Washington, Memorial Day weekend of 1991. It was one of those family togetherness weekends. We had visited Eastern Washington, checking a variety of interesting towns and cheap motels. Most of the time, the weather wasn't wonderful, but the weather is rarely noteworthy on Memorial Day weekend in Washington. Besides, hardy Northwesterners that we are, we would never let something as small as a few clouds spoil our good time.

The sun smiled on us as we pulled into the parking area of the lake. The sun continued to bless us as we pulled the box from our car bearing the picture of three happy people in an inflatable raft. We hauled the box to the edge of the lake and the sun dipped behind a cloud. More clouds gathered as we inflated our new toy. The sky was completely gray as we hoisted our $29.99-on-sale raft onto our shoulders and stood at the boat launch behind the people with a $20,000 boat.

Ah, family togetherness! I took videos as Dad and children, encased in orange life preservers, rowed in circles and waved. "Goodbye! We're off to explore the island in the middle of the lake."

They made it to the island as the first rain drops hit. I watched from shore and imagined the conversation on that little piece of rock:

"It's raining. Gross!"

"Quick! Get in the boat. Be careful. Sit down!"

"I'm wet!"

"SIT DOWN!"

By the time the happy adventurers were half-way back I could hardly see them through the sheet of rain. When they finally reached shore, no one was smiling.

"Wait 'til I get out," my husband commanded his fellow drowned rats.

"Will you sit still!" he snarled at squirming Junior, who looked like a miniature raincloud, himself.

Junior was temporarily out of favor with father. As was THE BOAT, which had sprung a leak halfway back.

"Water!" Junior had shrieked and begun to wiggle dangerously, bringing yet more water into the leaking vessel.

"We won't drown," Dad had assured him. "That's why we're wearing these life preservers."

Junior paid no attention to his life preserver. He was too busy squirming and watching the water seeping around him. Silly child. His father was with him. They were already halfway back before the boat had started to leak, and he was wearing a life preserver.

It was all very amusing. When it was someone else. But one week later, home again . . .

My friends, Sam and Sue Songwriter, were due in from Nashville. A mutual friend had already met them at the airport. The last time they'd visited, I had been responsible for getting them to and from the airport. When picking them up I'd enjoyed a flat tire, and when I was to take them back, the car had refused to start.

But I had no airport pressures this time. My friend, Jonsey, had Sam and Sue right now. After a few days, Jonsey would put them on the Edmonds-Kingston ferry and I would drive twenty miles to the town of Kingston to pick them up. No problem. I could hardly wait for my company.

Three days before they were to arrive, I jumped into my trusty rusty rattler only to discover it wouldn't start. Dead battery. All right. History would not repeat itself. When hubby got home I would send him out for a new battery.

The new battery was installed and voila! The car started again. "Maybe you should get it to the shop and have it checked," suggested hubby. "Something could be wrong with the charging system."

I knew what that meant—charging system, as in, "If this system doesn't work the battery won't either." I called the shop the next morning in a panic. "It's an emergency."

"Well," drawled the mechanic. "I can fit you in bright and early tomorrow morning."

Tomorrow morning. The same day the company was due. "How early?" I asked.

"Eight a.m." he assured me.

"Eight a.m." I repeated, comforted.

Here's how Company-Day progressed:

7:55 a.m. My sick car and I arrive at the shop.

8:00 a.m. No mechanic is on duty.

8:15 a.m. Still no mechanic. I peer in the garage windows.

Nope. No mechanic is inside.

8:30 a.m. I am pacing and peering in windows again. This does not produce a mechanic. I vow that when he does show up I'll throttle him with a radiator hose.

8:35 a.m. The owner of the garage arrives and I inform him that he has no mechanic.

8:36 a.m. The owner agrees. Nope. No mechanic. I smile and grind my teeth.

8:40 a.m. The owner has unlocked all the doors, started the coffee and pulled the sick car into the examination room. I follow and hover.

8:55 a.m. The owner says, "Well, it looks pretty good."

"Great!" I exclaim, and use his phone to call Jonsey. "Put Sam and Sue on the 9:15 ferry," I instruct. "I'll meet them."

9:00 a.m. I return to the examination room. "Uh oh," says the owner from under the hood.

"Uh oh? What's the matter?" Don't panic!

"You'll need a new alternator or you'll have another dead battery," announces the owner, holding up what looks like a metal heart for Frankenstein's bride. The thought of having a dead battery and being stuck somewhere between Kingston and the island strikes terror in my heart.

"I can have it done by 2:30 this afternoon," promises the nice man.

"OK." I call over my shoulder, dashing for the phone.

9:01 a.m. I grab the phone and call my buddy, Island Annie.

"Help! I have a sick car and I have to meet my company at the ferry."

"OK," says Annie. "Don't panic. Little Annie and I will just pop 'round to the garage and pick you up. We'll go to little Annie's ballet lesson and then fetch your friends."

"Thank you," I breathe.

9:02 a.m. I call Jonesy's house again to tell Jonsey to put Sue and Sam on the next ferry. Too late. No answer. Sam and Sue are already being shuttled to the ferry.

Oh, no! What will Sam and Sue do when they arrive in Kingston and I don't meet them? Will they panic and get back on the ferry? Will they be mad? Will Jonsey be mad if Sam and Sue come back and she has to go get them? And here's a new horrible thought: What if Sue and Sam get back on the other side of the water and don't have Jonsey's phone number? Is Jonsey in the phone book?

What to do? Call the ferry dock!

9:05 a.m. I reach the toll booth at the ferry dock. I beg the ticket man to pass on my life-and-death message. "You can't miss these people," I say. "She's short. He's tall and has gray hair."

The ticket man latches onto the word gray. "Oh. Are they old?"

"Old? No, they aren't old. Sam is prematurely gray." (Like I'm becoming!) "They talk with southern accents," I continue. "You can't miss them." I hang up, hoping that's true.

9:25 a.m. When Island Annie rescues me, I'm pacing in front of the garage, trying to convince myself everything will be all right.

9:45 a.m. I'm sitting in the proud mama section at the dance school, watching future ballerinas hop around behind their teacher. Nerves, or something, are hopping in my veins, making them tingle. I want to scream, but keep my lips clamped tightly in a fake smile.

10:10 a.m. Annie and I race from the dance school to Annie's van.

10:15 a.m. Annie speeds down the highway. She passes me a granola bar. When nervous, eat.

10:45 a.m. Annie and I arrive in Kingston. The 9:15 boat from Edmonds has come and gone. A new boat is already emptied and now loading. The 10:50 is about to leave. I see no sign of Sue and Sam. More panic. Did they give up on me and get back on the ferry? Should I run to the boat and tear around the deck looking for them? The boat will leave in five minutes. What if I go on it to search for the missing songwriters and don't get off in time? Would Annie wait for me to return? And if Annie did wait, would she be angry? How could this mess have happened?

I'm ready to buy a sword and fall on it when the coffee shop by the ferry dock comes into focus. Maybe, just maybe . . .

Oh, thank you, Lord! There they are. Never getting the message I left at the ferry dock and too confused to know what to do, Sam and Sue Songwriter went for coffee.

I rush inside. "Thank God I found you!" I gush, remembering who had picked up all the dropped threads as the morning unraveled.

* * *

All that panicking for nothing. All that energy wasted in wringing hands and moaning. I was wearing my life jacket all along but, like my son, I could only see the water in my boat. And that was just a minor incident!

How many needless worries have I nurtured over the years? I remember the report card that launched me into orbit as I envisioned Honey sliding from "Ds" in every vital subject to a life on the streets, unable to care for herself or function in society.

Then there was Honey's social life. Every little tiff with her friends was enlarged in my mind to World War II proportions, and I worried that she'd have no friends and be scarred for life.

Every time Junior got sick I fought with the spectre of a fatal disease. What if something were to happen to Junior, my only son? "Sufficient unto the day is the evil thereof." How true. I have enough to occupy my mind and energy by working on one problem at a time. I don't need to multiply them and project them into the future.

Remember the example of the sparrow? asked my Father.

I had read Matthew 10:29 often enough over the past twenty years. I nodded.

If I am concerned enough with my creation to even care about the death of a sparrow, doesn't it make sense I will be concerned with every area of your life? Your finances aren't the only area where you can stop worrying. Trust Me with the other things too.

The Father, very kindly, didn't add, *And how many times have we gone over this very basic lesson?*

I thought again of First Peter 5:7, which tells us to give all of our cares to our Lord. I realized that advice is backed by a good reason. God is the only one capable of handling those things beyond our control: the layoffs, the unexpected illnesses, the ups and downs of the economy.

If Jesus could find a coin in a fish, He can surely show me how to find the things my family needs during a bad economy. He can even show me how to find lost houseguests!

When the unexpected and the unwanted happen I need to practice the advice in First Corinthians 10:5. I need to capture every wild, panicky, we're-all-gonna-die thought galloping around in my brain and throw it out. I have to actually say, "I'm not going to worry about that."

Then I must distract my brain, asking it to think in other ways, about other things—such as problem solving instead of problem inventing. "What can I do to help this situation?" If I can do nothing to help, I can probably do something to make myself feel better about the problem or to help my family cope with it. Worrying is not an option. If nothing is truly too big for my Father to handle, then I have no reason to panic.

Here, said my Father. *I'll make it even simpler. Think of this lesson as the Three P's. First, PRAY. Pray for guidance before you begin any project. Sometimes you rush into things I don't want you to do at all. If you pray about it first I can guide you. I can open and shut doors of circumstance as well as doors in your mind. I can help you know when to say "yes" and when to say "no." I can assure you that you're doing the right thing. Pray when things go wrong. I can still help, even when you've muddled it.*

Second, think ahead. PLAN for potential problems and devise a plan "B." If you are expected somewhere and your car is acting up, let someone know when you're leaving and what your expected route is. That way if you break down, after a reasonable time, they'll come look for you. Or, take the bus. With a plan "B" you won't panic when plan "A" fails.

And speaking of plan "B"s, isn't it time you started that savings account you've talked about for so long? You know, the one for emergencies?

Oh, yes. That account. The Father is right. SAVE should not be a four-letter word, but a way of life. If God hadn't showed Joseph a plan to store grain for the coming seven years of famine, the people of Egypt and his own family (the future nation of Israel) would have starved. I need something stored in savings for times of financial famine.

Third, continued the Father, *PUT worries from your mind. Refuse to let them spin your head and eat your stomach lining. Quote My Word to calm yourself. Then resort to step one.*

"What was step one?"

Pray. Remember?

I blushed. "Oh, yeah."

The Three P's, huh? I thought about it.

I'm still thinking about it, and the day my son and I sat in the doctor's office, waiting to see X-rays of his foot, I tried practicing it. I almost cried,

but instead, I waited to hear if the mysterious ail-
ment causing him so much pain was fatal. Junior
and I played twenty questions to occupy our
minds.

The problem turned out not to be fatal—something with a long Latin name which he'll outgrow.
That was good news.

So was the discovery that the Three P's works.
Mother and son left the doctor's office, both wearing smiles.

"I think I'm learning my lesson," said Mom,
then added, "I think I have a great teacher!"

Chapter 12

Tacos and Manna—
A One-Act Morality Play

Act One, Scene One:

A bright, cheery kitchen. Mom hums as she sets the table. Dinner simmers on the stove. Enter Junior.

Junior: What's for dinner?

Mom: Tacos.

Junior: Not tacos again! Yuck.

Mom: Tacos are your father's favorite.

Junior: I'm sick of tacos. Why can't we have something else?

Mom: I just told you; tacos are your father's favorite, and we're having what he likes tonight.

Junior stomps off in disgust. Mom frowns. Fade.

Act One, Scene Two:

We are still in the same kitchen. Mom is at the stove, stirring a pot. Enter Junior.

Junior: Hi, Mom. What's for dinner?

Mom: Potato soup and French bread.

Junior: Potato soup. (In dejected tones) When can we have pizza?

Mom: Soon.

Junior exits, frowning, stage left. Fade.

Act One, Scene Three:

Mom is still in the kitchen. It is bright but not so cheery. Mom is not humming. Enter Junior.

Junior, watching Mom roll out pie crust: Oh, boy! Are we having pie?

Mom: Meat pie. Chicken pot pie, to be exact.

Junior: Any pie for dessert?

Mom: We've had way too much junk lately. No dessert tonight.

Junior: We haven't had dessert in months. When will we have dessert?

End of Scene Three. Mom brings the curtain down on Junior.

* * *

The quickest way for a child to drive a mother crazy is to squawk about dinner. The poor woman is doing her best to balance the four food groups, keep her family from getting high blood pressure or cancer of the colon, watch their fat intake and provide variety and a good taste experience all at the same time. And on a budget. No easy order to fill. What mother doesn't see red when one of her offspring frowns and pushes the fruits of her labor around his plate? I say every mother has a right to righteous indignation when this happens. Ingratitude is crummy!

Any woman who has slaved over an unappreciated meal can imagine how the heavenly Father felt when His children complained about the manna they were served in the wilderness.

Manna was a mysterious, seedlike substance which daily fell like dew on the ground for the nomadic nation of Israel as they traveled from slavery in Egypt to freedom in the land God had promised them. This was a real multipurpose food. The people could boil it in pots or cook it into cakes. It was tasty no matter how they cooked it.

But someone in Egypt had told them variety was the spice of life. "All we get is this crummy manna. We're sick of this stuff," they complained (Numbers 11:6). This was God's provision, yet they complained. Imagine that! What ingratitude . . .

"I don't have anything to wear. What I'd give for some new clothes." . . . "Is it asking too much to want a decent car?" . . . "By our age, shouldn't life be easier? Shouldn't we make more money?" . . .

I thought of tacos and manna and ingrates—
both Jewish and Gentile, young and old. When I
complained, was I behaving any differently than
my son? Oh, we each sang a different verse, but it
was the same old song, the same song of discontent the Israelites sang a few thousand years ago.

Paul warned the Corinthian church about ingratitude (1 Corinthians 10:1-11), using the nation
of Israel as an example. This first generation of
God's people was protected by God's presence,
the pillar of cloud, as they left captivity and followed Moses across the Red Sea. As they plunged
through the parting waters, they probably didn't
realize they were being symbolically baptized into
a new life of freedom. In that new life, a daily pic-
nic of manna was spread out on the ground for
them. In the desert they miraculously received
water from a rock. Everything they needed was
provided during the hard times. And the best still
lay ahead. Yet they grumbled. Like my son. Like
me.

Their grumbling resulted in the punishment of
suffering and death. More grumbling and lack of
faith and a whole generation missed settling in the
land God had promised. What promised land do I
miss every time I complain?

Playing Monday morning quarterback, I wonder why they thought the manna was so bad. Because I'm studying someone else's behavior, the
answer is obvious: comparison. The Jewish people
compared camp life to what they had in Egypt.
Like many of us moving toward the promised

land, they lost sight of their goal and wrapped the past in a sentimental mist. "Oh, for the goodies we had in Egypt. We used to eat so well!" The Israelites may have eaten well, but they were still slaves. Captives.

Not any more. Now they headed to something great, to the land of milk and honey.

On the way to a terrific life, there isn't always time for luxuries or splendid banquets. When you travel, you travel lightly. When you're camping, you eat camp food. Mountain climbers eat gorp en route to the summit. They know it isn't their main meal, but it will nourish them until they reach their camp site.

The Israelites were not happy campers because they forgot they were in transit, on their way to important things. Instead of looking to what lay ahead, they concentrated on their present discomfort.

Just like I do. Instead of being grateful for the provisions I've received, I grumble because it's not what I want. "Tacos again?"

The Father knew what His people needed for traveling fast and He gave it to them.

He does the same for me. I may think I have time for those fancy goodies Madison Avenue dangles before my face. But most of those pretty toys cost a lot money. And making that much money costs a lot of time. And if I give all my time to acquiring those things, am I dreaming of Egypt or the Promised Land?

I look at my oldest daughter, Dolly, who is

trapped for a lifetime in a body that functions on the level of a four-month old. She has cause for complaint.

But Dolly rarely complains. If her stomach is empty, she lets me know. If she's sick, I hear about it. Otherwise she contentedly sits in her wheelchair and watches cartoon images skitter across the television screen or, on a nice day, she sits outside and laughs when the breeze tickles her face. She never complains that she's worn the same dumb outfits for the last three months. She never whines for new toys. The same old ones keep her happy. And if she gets bored with them, she's content to chew her fingers. And food? "Hey, just feed me! I'll be happy with almost anything you want to put in my mouth."

After twenty years, sometimes I still look at Dolly and cry.

Then I have to ask, Who am I crying for—her or me? She's happy. She's content with her life. If she, who seems to have so little, can be so happy, how much more should I, who has so very much, be happy?

God has provided for me. He's carefully provided only what I need so the things I want won't tangle me and hinder my journey. What I want is lobster or steak. What I get is tacos. I think about Dolly and say, "Hey, tacos beat starving."

I think of my son, always looking on the stove wishing for something different. How like his mother! I guess the next time he complains, I'll say to him what I'm coming to realize myself:

"What does it really matter what's on the stove as long as we eat it in an atmosphere of love, as long as we're healthy and happy and staying on the road to the Promised Land?"

DISTINGUISHING NEED FROM GREED

Chapter 13

Where Do They Get It?

"Mom! Junior took a can of pineapple juice for his lunch and I asked him not to because that's my favorite kind."

"Honey, you have six cans. Can't you share one?"

"But that's my favorite! Can't he drink the apple juice?" . . .

"Mom! Junior stole a piece of my candy bar!"

"How do you know?"

"Because I cut it in six pieces. Now I only have five."

"I didn't!" Junior insists (tearfully, and with a mouth oozing chocolate). "There were only five pieces." . . . "Mom! Honey stole my . . . Hey! Give it!"

"I'm just looking at it. Mom!" . . .

I talk until I'm blue in the face, but this selfish behavior keeps popping up—like a weed. Why are my children so selfish? Where do they get it? . . .

"No. You may not have my Diet Coke. I'm the one who's dieting. . . . Not now, I'm busy (doing something for me, which is more important than doing something for you!). . . . Just because I'm having a cookie, does that mean you need one, too? I swear, if I were eating my last meal on earth you'd want the last bite. . . . A Christmas gift for the pastor? Give me a break. He already makes twice as much as my husband. Anyway, I'll be lucky if my money stretches enough to buy Christmas gifts for my own family. . . ."

"The selfish behavior of my offspring isn't entirely my fault," I reasoned after my past comments replayed. "After all, they inherited the same genetic handicap I did—sin."

But the Father didn't buy that excuse. *If you want your children to master unselfishness shouldn't you be more careful about what kind of a role you model? Maybe,* He continued, *you need to look more closely at the things you call yours.*

"I don't understand."

Think a minute.

Certain phrases sprung to mind, like "my time." I have always guarded that time jealously and am often irritated at interruptions like early school dismissals and telephone calls. How often had I gritted my teeth and tried to be pleasant to a talkative friend on the phone when ire hopped in my mind like a demon, screaming, "I have things to do!" But on the other end of the phone, a woman clutched her receiver like a life preserver, dying for adult contact.

She wasn't the only one I brushed aside in my scurrying. How many times had I rushed through devotions because I had "things to do"?

If you are My servant, whose time do you hoard so carefully for your own projects and pleasures? wondered the Father.

Good question. I didn't have an anwer. Well, I did, but I didn't want to give it.

I thought about Jesus' public ministry. He didn't seem at all concerned about time management, and He never appeared rushed. He seemed to spend much time walking around talking to people. He hung around the temple; He went to people's homes; He taught; He healed. He didn't write His memoirs. Was it because He knew God would take care of that? He didn't own a home. Maybe that was because He'd seen the heavenly mansions and knew nothing could compare. Or did He know it would drain too much precious time from the really important things?

And speaking of time, our Lord wasn't possessive of His hours, either. Nowhere in Scripture do we read Him saying, "Not today. I'm busy." He didn't take time off from His ministry to putter with a little carpentry project. He had no hobbies, "interests" or distractions. The only time He took for Himself was time to spend alone with the Father.

How very unlike me, I thought.

Time isn't all I like to grab for myself. I do like to take the last cookie ("After all, I made them") or the spare ten bucks in the checkbook ("I haven't had anything new in ages").

"I deserve this" is another favorite phrase. I say it to myself and to my friends. "Oh, go ahead. Don't feel guilty. You deserve it." How many times have I overspent my budget while rationalizing like the lady in the commercial, "I'm worth it. I deserve it."

I sighed, murmuring, "It's all rather depressing and discouraging."

But not hopeless, said my Father. *We can work on this. I'll give you strength. Where would you like to start?*

"Well, I guess Junior can have the last swallow of my Diet Coke."

Yes. What else?

"He can have a cookie too."

Prodding silence.

"I suppose I could spare ten dollars for the pastor's Christmas bonus." I thought a moment. "On second thought, could we make that five?"

Chapter 14

The Christmas Blues

During Christmas vacation one year, Honey and Junior came home from playing with Di-Di and Do-Do. "Di-Di got a water bed for Christmas," said Honey.

"Do-Do has his own TV," Junior announced.

I felt a mixture of emotions: disgust with the children's parents, who were obviously trying to buy the kids' affections; wonder that these people could afford so many expensive trinkets; and envy that I couldn't do the same.

Like the ghost of Christmas past, Guilt paid a visit, making me regret choices made years earlier. It whispered that I was a rotten mother.

I agreed. I told myself I should get a full-time job so I'd have more money to spend on my children. If I had done so years earlier, my darlings could have kept up with the junior Joneses.

My poor, deprived babies. They missed so many things in their young lives. What would this do to their self-esteem?

I mused on these worries with a friend the day after New Year's Day. "Nonsense," she snapped, giving me the familiar lecture about it being more important to give time to our children. "The family that plays together . . . Your children are under great pressure and need you home and available when they have problems. You couldn't do any volunteer work if you got a job."

I left my friend's house feeling it was more important to remain a close family than to search for more money and things. After all, I realized, I'd heard many adults fondly reminisce about impoverished, love-filled childhoods, but I had never heard anyone say, "We didn't have much love, but we always had lots of things."

This cozy, Walton-family feeling lasted two weeks, until my kids went back to school and saw what others got for Christmas. Then the warm fuzzies went down the drain. *Why do my children want so much, anyway?* I questioned grumpily.

Could it be they've spent too much time listening to their mother? I look through magazines and drool. I sit in front of the television and hunger to be like that rich romance novelist I saw in a mystery movie. Never mind the fact that she got murdered. I want what she had: a huge house with oyster-colored carpet, a luxury car, French underwear.

After visiting others, I tell my heavenly Father, "Harriet has a new car. She wore another gorgeous outfit. I want new clothes. And a Hawaiian vacation. I want a glistening, all white kitchen like Harriet has, and French undies. I want . . ."

What do you really want? asks my Father. *Why do you ask for these things?*

The answer is hard to put my finger on. "I want to be happy," I finally conclude.

Will those things make you happy?

"Oh, I've heard that before," I reply cynically.

Well, will they?

"Yes!"

For how long will they make you happy? How long before the newness wears off your pretty, big house with the oyster-colored carpet? How long before it becomes nothing more than what it is—shelter, a place to eat and sleep and entertain your friends? That happened when you bought your suburban home. Remember?

I squirm uncomfortably and my Father continues, *Remember how you walked around your shiny new house in awe, hardly able to believe it was yours? Remember how you thanked Me for such a wonderful house? But after a while, your enthusiasm waned, and you realized your house, pretty as it was, couldn't sustain your happiness.*

Let's talk clothes. I could give you a new, expensive wardrobe. How long before your pretty clothes would be out of style?

I am, by now, becoming a fast learner, and the Father doesn't need to point out that this conversation is similar to the one I had with my children after they returned from Di-Di and Do-Do's house.

Man-made treasures are cheap. My treasures are indestructible. Which do you really want to acquire? Which do you want for your children?

Naturally, I want the best, which means my son won't have a television in his bedroom until he has his own apartment. As it is we all spend too much time worshiping at the throne of the electric cyclops.

And my daughter? The closest she'll come to a water bed is if she douses hers with a hose.* I'll probably never spend a fortune on her wardrobe, either, which means she'll have to compensate for not looking radically peerlike and develop a wonderful personality instead.

The checking account will probably always be low, but maybe we can compensate by spending time with our children and filling our memory banks.

I'm realizing that greed is a form of lust. Just as lust for another person separates us from our mate, so lust for all the toys of our culture separates us from God. We think about the new attractions constantly. We sacrifice to get them and spend our spare time with them. No wonder James compared greedy Christians to unfaithful spouses (4:4).

I'm also seeing that greed is a feeling that can't grow unless it's fed by my attention. The longer I look at something, the stronger its pull.

That expensive dress in a store window is merely bait to lure the shopper inside. And I bite

---

*   Author's note: Futons are the rage now, and after Honey's bed collapsed, we got her a futon and turned her into a trendsetter. Everything comes to she who waits.

for the bait if I stare at it, long for it, imagine myself in it and wonder how I could get it. Once I have obsessesed over it, it has turned from simply a lovely dress into an object of desire. And I am in danger of being reeled into the store where, in moments I'll be parted from my money.

I have control over where my eyes focus. I don't have to browse through catalogues or window shop—pastimes that tend to feed my greed. (Nor do I need to keep toy catalogues around the house to tempt my children.)

When I do run errands, I may be less susceptible to impluse buying if I take a shopping list and resolve to stick to it. I have a friend who only shops for items on her list. If a store isn't on her list, she doesn't stop. Heaven only knows how many bargains she's missed . . . or how much money she's saved.

If I put myself on a schedule and only allow a certain amount of time to run errands I'll be less inclined to dawdle at sale racks or to browse. The little fish who stops to admire the pretty worm gets caught!

When this little fish does get caught, I find I can lure myself out of the store by telling myself I'll return next week when I'm not so busy or on pay day or after I've lost ten pounds (which is a sure guarantee I'll buy no more clothing the rest of my life). Once away from the appealing object—whether it's a dress or lawn furniture—the fever leaves. I decide the item I couldn't live without is not worth returning for or I realize I can't afford it.

Want is a funny feeling. It can't live long in an environment lacking encouragement. I don't want what I'm not focusing on. If I turn my focus onto the things that bring personal satisfaction—my family and friends, my church duties—I'm less likely to be discontent.

I still like perfume and nice clothes, fancy lingerie and oyster-colored carpet. But nice as these things are, I know they won't affect my long-range happiness any more than than a TV or water bed will complete my children's lives. In fact, like my children, many of the items I want are nothing more than spiritual junk food.

I've figured myself out, but I wonder how I can wean my kids off material Twinkies. How can I shift their focus from material goodies to more sustaining emotional and spiritual goodies?

My Father and I begin to brainstorm. *When the holidays come why not deemphasize presents and concentrate on an occasion?* suggests the Father.

Yes! I could fill our Christmas season with more experiences and less shopping, put fewer presents under the tree and do more people-oriented activities. I could take the kids caroling or let them bake Christmas cookies for their friends or for those in nursing homes. We could start some new family rituals.

"A Christmas short-story project!" I exclaim. "The kids could write a short story about a Bible character involved with Christ's birth—how that person might have felt, how Jesus's birth changed his life."

Or a story telling how My Son's birth has affected your child's life or the life of a friend, suggests the Father.

"Complete with art work," I add. "Junior and Honey are both good at art."

Now I'm really enjoying this change of focus. "And birthdays," I continue. "Perhaps we could buy Junior that new bike at some time other than his birthday. We could get him something small but nice that will emphasize his worth. I could buy him writing materials or art supplies or that children's Bible.

"And this year would be a good year to follow a friend's example and make each child a flag, complete with personalized emblem. Then every following year we can fly each child's flag on his or her birthday, graduation, whatever. Junior likes sharks and loves to play baseball. I could put a shark in the middle, maybe a baseball in the corner. And Honey loves cats. I could put a kitty on hers."

Mom's on a roll now. "I could pick a special Bible verse for the year for each child's birthday, maybe even frame it," I continue. "I can alleviate the material haul and load the kids with attention and self-esteem builders!"

Great ideas! My mind is buzzing as more schemes fill my head. I'm excited, and almost hoping my family will follow my example and do the same things for me. . . .

I suppose next Christmas I'll still put expensive perfume and French undies on my wish list. And, despite my efforts, my kids will ask for the Oakland Raiders and stock in Disneyland. But maybe we won't want things as desperately. Maybe we'll have a nice Christmas in spite of what we don't get.

> Do not store up for yourselves treasures on earth, where moth and rust destroy, and where thieves break in and steal. But store up for yourselves treasures in heaven, where moth and rust do not destroy, and where thieves do not break in and steal. For where your treasure is, there your heart will be also. (Matthew 6:19-21)

Chapter 15

Big Woman on Campus

It seems like yesterday when my daughter and I had our holiday "so-and-so has" conversation. However, it was many yesterdays ago. So many that I thought my daughter was the most together teenager in America. So secure, so confident, so content. Then, at fourteen . . .

Be it ever so humble no place is like home—especially when two females who live there are fighting. At first I thought the roaring and screaming was simply over doing the dishes, something Honey hates nearly as much as homework. But I learned the truth later at bedtime (such a good time to have these conversations—everyone is so rested, so emotionally stable).

The real problem behind the slamming of pots and pans and long face was Honey's best friend's Christmas present. Angel received her very own CD player. And for her fourteenth birthday, the day after Christmas, Angel got a leather jacket.

And Angel wasn't the only one with such wonders. According to Honey, all her friends had the important things in life: CD players, boom boxes, personal phone lines, an entire jacket wardrobe. She didn't. And Angel, who had it all, was popular.

"Maybe it's because she's nice," I suggested.

How could I be so dense? Angel's possessions were what made her so well-liked. As for poor Honey, no one liked her. Our impoverished lifestyle created her social ruin. Without proper accessories how could she be popular?

I vainly point out the good things Honey had: a house with her own private woods and beach, two parents who loved her and each other and spent hours playing games with her. "Do your friends' parents spend time with them or have parties for them?"

"Yes," Honey assured me. "They can have parties whenever they want. Their parents are always available for them. And they all have CD players."

Mature woman that I am, I told my daughter how ungrateful she was and stormed off to cry and scream at my heavenly Father. "If we made more money I could buy Honey more cool clothes. We could go to Disneyland. We're not asking too much to go to Disneyland, are we? After all, Honey's best friend just went on a Carribean cruise. I'm not asking for that. Just Disneyland. Other people have a lot. Why can't we? My husband's smart. Why can't he earn more?"

My mind drifted to visions of myself in fancy new clothes (visions I'd had a lot lately. Also, in this vision I was twenty pounds lighter, but that's beside the point). In my imagination, I strolled out the door of my large, perfectly furnished house and climbed into a new, metallic blue car with jazzy lines—one without the dashboard chewed up.

The vision evaporated with a "poof" as I discovered I was thinking like my daughter, only on a larger scale. Good heavens! Could more than one ungrateful daughter be in this house?

My mind replayed a tape from the evening news about people in all those struggling countries that once were Russia. They had been fighting over food, chopping limbs from trees in parks so they could have firewood to heat their homes. Were they worrying about having the latest toys or being popular?

The world, and the media, say the best and most successful people have more. Even those of us who should know better believe them. If we have more, we reason that everyone will know how talented we are. Riches prove our worth. Without those riches, without the trappings to label us, we feel we're nothing.

But with the trappings, how do I know if people are interested in me or simply in my possessions? If all I can offer someone is myself, at least I know why that person wants to be my friend.

I remember once when someone complimented me. I cynically retorted, "If I'm so talented, why am I so broke?"

The person looked shocked by my stupidity. "Artists are never appreciated in their lifetimes," she informed me.

The same applies for ordinary, good people. They have to wait until their funeral to find how much everyone loved them, because no one realizes how important those average good people are until they're gone. No one sees how much they contributed to others' lives until their absence leaves a gaping hole.

Ben and Marliss Moyle are two of those ordinary, good people. They raised five children on a tight budget, then opened their home to foster children. Now that they've retired they're busy with community volunteer work. They still have no money and no status, but their community would be poor without them.

The average trying-the-best-I-can type person doesn't always get rich—at least not in the world's eyes. But James 2:5 assures us that person will be rich in something far more important: faith.

And such a person usually isn't friendless either. Most of us find acceptance even if we don't make a six-figure income. We find friends who value us for what we are.

If I have friends who value me for myself, why do I entertain visions of myself adorned with new trimmings?

Maybe, like my daughter, I need to take stock of myself. Am I worth knowing just as I am? Am I kind to others? Fun to be with? A dependable and loyal friend? Can I keep a confidence?

If my daughter and I can answer "yes" to these questions, we don't need as much as we think we do.

MOM'S LESSONS IN LANGUAGE ARTS

I believe the purpose of language arts is for the student to learn to communicate through written and spoken word, and to understand the communications of others.

In junior high, I read Shakespeare and learned to spell long words I haven't used since.

In high school, I tried to write poetry that would make my teacher smile and say, "Brilliant!" And I learned more long words.

In college I studied poems I would never understand and read depressing stories by famous modern writers— trying to discover why my professors said they were great. Now words were really long.

Nobody taught me how to spell them. Instead, my instructors used them and assumed I understood. I only understood that I often didn't understand.

But the lessons my children have given me in this subject make those college courses look easy. The Father worked with me on my vocabulary, and now I'm finding that words I've known since childhood have gleaned a whole new meaning.

COMMUNICATION

Chapter 16

Are You
Listening to Me?

We were at the beach. Honey, then six, and little brother Junior had enjoyed an afternoon of racing up and down tide flats, climbing rocks and playing tag with waves. Now it was time to go home. Dolly was hungry. I was tired.

I called to Honey, who was down the beach, climbing on another rock. "Come on, Honey. Time to go home."

Honey developed a hearing problem and scampered further down the beach.

I trotted after her, Junior and Dolly in tow, still patiently calling, "Time to go home."

Honey still couldn't hear, so I picked up speed. She sprinted too, but even with my two handicaps, I was faster. I swooped down on my daughter, grabbed her by the arm and firmly towed.

"Perhaps the problems which often arise between mother and offspring are due to a lack of communication," a child psychologist might suggest.

I don't think so. I think in instances like this one, both mother and child communicated quite clearly. "You will," said Mom.

"I won't," said the child.

We both know what the problem is, but that doesn't stop my children from pretending they can't understand English.

I say, "No more cookies," and when I catch Junior with crumbs on his hands and bulging cheeks, he looks mystified by my anger.

"Huh?" he says.

"Use your knife and fork," I say. Fingers are easier. Junior pretends he doesn't know what tableware is.

Honey smuggles the cat into her room to help her make her bed (which, of course, means the bed will take longer to make than the building of Rome). "No. Take that cat out of your room and put her down," says Mom. Honey obeys only the last part of the sentence, but when scolded says, "I thought you said . . . "

Grrr . . .

* * *

"This deliberate lack of understanding is a very bad habit," I mutter.

It certainly is, agrees the Father. *Remind you of anyone we know?*

My hand presses my chest dramatically. "Moi?"
Yes, you.

"You aren't holding one little incident against me, are You? After all, it was so long ago."

That particular incident was, agrees the Father. *You know I have forgiven you for deliberately misunderstanding and looking for a job after I instructed you to devote extra time to your family.*

I still remember how the Father got my attention by allowing me to become pregnant. Now that I look back on that experience, I chuckle. I can almost hear Him saying, *All right. She obviously doesn't think she has enough family to bother over. We can change that.* I gave up my job hunt.

That was then. This is now. "I haven't had a language problem in a long time," I say.

Has it been that long since this morning?

Oh, yes. This morning. I hadn't misunderstood the Father, but someone else. The incident was small, but indicated a flaw that needed to be corrected. I was playing tennis with the girls.

Something about being out with three other people puts me in a party mood. I want to laugh, make jokes and be silly. One of our players, however, is a serious athlete. For her, concentration is the name of the game.

As I giggled my way around the court, she dropped a couple of subtle hints that I conveniently didn't hear. Finally, after I shrieked over a particularly good shot from one of our opponents (which my partner missed), she smiled and said through clenched teeth, "Sheila, will you shut up?

You're distracting me and I can't hit the ball."

That got my attention. My red face communicated that I understood my friend perfectly.

Lack of understanding sometimes isn't a good enough excuse. So my children acquire temporary deafness. "Take out the garbage? When did you say that?" "Run the dishwasher? I didn't hear."

I used to see this a lot involving candy. Does this scenario sound familiar?

Child A has been at a friend's house. The sibling (Child B) and Mom pick up Child A. Then, as soon as Mom starts to drive home, Child A displays the bag of cavity rocks, a souvenier from the visit. Child B says to Child A, "Can I have one?"

Child A stares out the car window, pretending to have not heard the request.

Child B repeats the request. (*Surely she just didn't hear me.* He thinks hopefully.)

Child A still stares out the car window and takes another hasty bite of candy, knowing Mom will soon intervene on Child B's behalf.

"Please?" begs Child B.

Deafness continues until the roar of mother penetrates the fog of selfishness.

I notice that I do the same thing. I conveniently don't hear. Convenience is the bottom line. It is inconvenient for me to make a detour, so I don't hear when someone announces he or she needs a ride home from church. Someone talks about financial struggles and I don't hear the underlying plea for help because I don't want to part with any of my precious loot.

Sometimes my kids are so absorbed in their activities or thoughts that they truly don't hear what anyone says. If the TV is on, Honey is lost to us until someone turns it off. If she's reading a book she is equally lost.

I'm the same way. If I'm deep in thought, the kids must try a couple of times to get through to me. If I'm planning my week, listing errands, organizing a party or mapping my life goals, the Father also has difficulties making Himself heard.

I have discerned that my heavenly Father would like to use the same guidelines with me that I use when I want my children's attention. When dealing with them I follow the three well-known steps: Remove distraction, make eye contact and have the child repeat the instruction.

Remove Distraction

When the kids were small, I set aside favorite toys while giving instructions. For the same reason, the TV went off. Only moms can do two things at once. Kids can't watch "Bugs Bunny" or wind up their airplane and hear what Mom is saying at the same time.

I've discovered I don't hear any better than my kids when I'm distracted. My Father needs my undivided attention. My best time to be with Him is before the kids are awake to distract me. While I may visit with Him over the kitchen sink, that's not the best place for me to receive important instructions or corrections. I need time to mull over what I've read in my Bible. I need time to meditate. And I can't concentrate on my Father's words if the radio is blaring or if kids are squabbling and the phone is ringing.

Eye Contact

Eyes tell a lot. They tell a parent what is in the heart because they reflect defiance or repentance. And the eyes show when the ears are working. One pair of eyes looking into another shows concentration (hopefully) and a focused mind.

That's the kind of contact I need to make with my Father. I need to glue my spiritual eyes on Him, to focus in on His words. This is not easy. Like my children, at times I don't want to look into His face. I'm too ashamed. At other times, I just don't want to listen, but want to let my mind wander. So many times when I'm halfway through my prayer time, I find I'm not concentrating on the Lord and that I haven't been concentrating for some time. My thoughts have drifted to my plans for the day or to whatever book I've been reading.

I have to mentally pull myself back and refocus my eyes, because if I'm not looking at the Father I know I'm not listening.

Repeat It

"Now, what did I say?" I'll ask after a Mommy speech.

"Not to let go of your hand while crossing the street," repeats the child.

"And why shouldn't you do that?"

"Because I might get hit by a car."

"Very good." Now I know the information is in the computer, and has been replayed for me—proof that my child has reached some level of understanding.

"Thy word have I hid in mine heart, that I might not sin against thee" (Psalm 119:11, KJV). The words are put into the computer then repeated to make sure they are comprehended and filed in the proper memory banks. I can't use what's not in the computer. And misinformation isn't helpful either. Better to repeat that Scripture or thought out loud, to write it down and to share my thoughts with my Father and others. This helps me make sure I have it right.

Listening isn't easy. I'd rather talk than listen any day. And if someone asks for something I don't want to give or says something I don't want to hear, I'm strongly tempted to misunderstand or acquire deafness.

But I can overcome temptation or improve communication skills. Most important, I can get a new hearing aid: an obedient heart. With that, I'll be amazed at what I can hear and the difference it will make in my life.

Chapter 17

What Do You Say?

We started working on our children when they were toddlers. When the cookie, candy or birthday present was placed in their chubby little hands, I would prompt, "What do you say?"

"Thank you," the child parroted. I'd properly reinforce this good behavior with a pat on the head and a kiss or I'd comment, "That's a good boy."

This was a good deal. Junior and Honey got their cookie and I got the warm feeling that I was raising polite, perfect children.

Somewhere along the road to big kidhood, we lost it. Maybe I slacked off on the psychological conditioning too soon. Maybe I thought the kids had learned the lesson when they really hadn't. Maybe the kids just got lazy. Or maybe the kids and I got lazy. Whatever the reason, as Honey and Junior got older, it seemed we were back to prompting them. Especially Junior. "Did you thank Mrs. Cleaver for having you over?" "What do you say to Grandma?" "Excuse me, is this a restaurant? Am I a waitress?"

"Oh. Thanks, Mom."

Grrr.

All right. So we encountered a few lapses. "Most of the time they're close to perfect," I consoled myself.

In September a van of friends took a weekend trip to Canada. The experience was nearly as perfect as my children. One of the less-than-perfect times involved those magic words I had tried so hard to program into my little dears.

Junior forgot to use the magic words and I wasn't nearby to prompt him with the famous Mom phrase, "What do you say?"

Junior forgot what you say. One of our fellow travelers pointed out to me that Junior was not very appreciative.

Everyone knows about mother lions and their cubs. And most people know the similarities between feline females and human ones. I turned to my offspring's attacker and bared my claws, ready to defend my cub. "He's just a kid. He's not perfect." Grrrr.

Then my gaze focused on my son. My eyes narrowed and I felt like swiping at him with my paw—er, hand. I watched Junior's every move for the rest of the trip, determined to make him perfect in thirty-six hours, just to prove what I knew all along: Junior was too perfect!

Poor lion cub. Junior looked at me with confusion and horror each time he made a minor mistake and I growled at him.

Many months passed before the Father could bring up this subject with me. On New Year's Day, I sat facing another year and musing that time flies. In a Lear jet. In a rocket.

So much happened this last year. So much to be grateful for, whispered the small voice. *So many good things taken for granted.*

My words to my children echoed, "What do you say?" What do I say? Well, I do manage to catch the big things. The healings, the job provided after unemployment. But what about all the little treats—the cookies? The cookies make routine life special. I began to think of all the cookies I'd taken from my heavenly Father without a word of thanks.

My friends. When was the last time I thanked God for those pockets of fun tucked in between the chores and the laundry, for the friend who excitedly announced, "I looked at my calendar wrong. I can have tea tomorrow. Is the offer still open?" Or for the friend who gave me socks with little tennis rackets on them to match hers? Or for the friend who helped us wire our house? What about the friend who called during a bad snow storm to make sure we had heat and power!

When was the last time I thanked the Father for a nice day or a mild winter after two harsh ones? Every invitation to someone's home, every phone call, every sunny day amid a week of rain is a treat. How often in the last year did I take those cookies for granted?

What other things did I overlook? I looked at my children. I thought of the pearls of wisdom they had dropped in the last year. I saw peeks at their future character, glimmers of hope. I remembered our recent bout with the flu and a miserable Honey announcing, "If this is what it's like to be drunk, I know I'll never drink." An encouraging word for any teen's mother! Had I whispered a quick "thanks" to the Father for giving my daughter that insight?

I had a flu shot earlier this fall. And although it didn't save me from the nasty bug my daughter caught, it protected me from the more virulent strains and from days of horror.

I remember I grumbled when I went to the community senior center for the shot. I hate needles. But I hate the flu worse. And I'm blessed to live in a country where that needle can deliver me from sickness. How many third-world mothers would travel miles to face that needle!

I get so many small daily treats that many people in the world would beg for. It's almost impossible to list them—from high-tech conveniences to leisure time. Cookies every time I turn around.

"What do you say, Mom?"

I say I need to open my eyes and say, "Thank you, Father."

And lest that thank you become rote, I'll imagine my life without some of those treats. How can I show my thankfulness? Maybe this year I need to write thank-you notes to the Father and collect them in a journal, written proof of God's goodness in my life. I can show my appreciation by sending encouraging notes to those struggling with something I've endured. I can spend more time blessing as I've been blessed, helping another mother whose children are not as far down the child development road as mine are by babysitting or housecleaning.

I can put my check in the offering plate with a "Thank You," to the One who has richly blessed me. And when the money is tight, I can write that tithe check, not regretfully, but gratefully remembering how the Father has provided for me.

New Year's Day. As we climbed into our faithful car and putt-putted off to a Disney movie with the kids I thought of many of my friends. They were enduring the noise of roaring TV while their husbands were lost to them and gazing at screens showing men in tights scrambling around in the mud after an oblong ball.

I grinned. This was a good place to start. I whispered, "Thank You, Father, that my husband doesn't like football."

VOCABULARY

Chapter 18

I Can't

I opened the cupboard where pots and pans were supposed to be neatly stacked. An avalanche of metal and porcelain buried my feet. "Junior! I want these pots and pans put away correctly," I called (in my sweetest voice).

"I can't," wailed eight-year-old Junior.

"Yes, you can," I insisted. "You may not want to, but I know you can."

"Can't" and "won't." *How frequently my children say one when they mean another,* I thought.

Much like myself, I realized. "Gee, I'm sorry. I can't." . . . "I'd love to help if I could." . . .

Why do we disguise those "won'ts" as "can'ts"? Usually because we're dodging something unpleasant—either work, which challenges our laziness or commitment, which challenges our selfishness.

"I can't get this math," says Honey. "I can't put those dishes away," moans Junior. "I can't learn to balance the checkbook," says Mom.

Each of us is really saying, "I don't want to do that. It involves extra work and will take time from what I want to do. It's yucky!"

Selfishness disguised as helplessness is irritating. We all see through the person who claims difficult circumstances as an excuse for inaction.

I remember hearing an interesting discussion a few years ago. Woman A, a kept woman whose day consisted of TV soap operas, complained about her lack of money to Woman B. "Why don't you get a job?" suggested Woman B.

"I can't do that," said Woman A. "I have a child."

"But Daddy Big Bucks is home during the day," said Woman B. "He could watch Snookums while you work."

Woman A shook her head. "No. He wouldn't watch her. And besides, I couldn't get a job that would pay me more than I'm getting on government assistance."

"You could go to school and get some training," suggested Woman B, who had done just that.

"I don't want to work," said Woman A, admitting what Woman B had suspected all along. Woman B was disgusted and said so.

The real motive for Woman A's reluctance to work wasn't her desire to spend more time with her child. It wasn't an inability to qualify for a job. Woman A could have easily qualified for a good job, but her real motive for staying home was a love of her easy life. She'd settled into a comfortable nest and had no desire to go back into the cold, cruel world and fend for herself.

Perhaps she knew if she'd admitted as much in the beginning she would have suffered contempt from the other woman. Perhaps that's why she substituted the phrase "I can't" for "I don't want to."

Maybe that's why I often do the same thing myself. If I say, "I can't," someone may buy it and I'll escape judgement.

In some cases the phrase, "I can't" is valid. My children really can't do some things. I can't ask fourteen-year-old Junior to hop into the Honda and run to the store for me. As much as he'd love to, he'd have to respond, "I can't, Mom. I don't know how to drive."

We just shouldn't expect some things of our children. Toddlers can't make a bed. Small children can't stay up late and still function well at school the next day. And older kids, even though they look capable, still don't have an adult grasp of life and shouldn't be in situations where they need it.

At times I've expected more of my children than they were capable of performing. Sometimes I've goofed and tried to coax a five-year-old into behaving like a nine-year-old or I've expected a ten-year-old's attention span from a three-year-old. Any request for a child to do something of which he's incapable should be met with the words, "I can't." After all, even Moms make mistakes occasionally and need to be made aware of those mistakes.

But what about reasonable requests? Wouldn't it be refreshing if they were answered honestly? Irritating, but refreshing.

Of course, I understand why my children prefer "can't" to "won't." They know such phrases as, "I don't want to" or "I don't feel like it" aren't acceptable responses to parental requests. "I can't," on the other hand, offers a chance to be let off the hook.

I guess that's why I occasionally try the same trick. Who do I think I'm fooling when I mumble my excuses? Surely not God. He knows when I'm truly too tired and when I'm just looking for an excuse to read my new library book. He knows when I really can't fit one more person in my car and when I just don't want to drag an extra kid along on an outing.

It's better to be honest in the first place because excuses don't work. If I'm trying to weasel out of something I should be doing I'll either feel rotten if I succeed or, if it's something really important, the Father will make sure I eventually do it anyway. Or worse yet, He'll let me lose an opportunity, turning blessedness into "blessedless."

Working things out is always easier when the heart is honest. At least you know where you stand. The kid in the youth group who says, "That idea stinks!" is, in the long run, easier to work with than the one who makes excuses for not participating in an activity or who complains about the way things are done and stays away. How can you work with that kid? How can you make your program more effective?

Making excuses is easy, especially if we're having serious problems. Rather than be honest with those who want to help, we let embarrassment motivate us into excusing ourselves out of sight and, hopefully, out of mind. "We're all so busy right now. We just can't make it to church." . . . "Well, you know, we've all had colds this last month."

Maybe it's true that the whole family has had colds or been busy. But perhaps colds and activities are being used as a cover-up because a person doesn't want to admit that she and her husband are having problems or that a child is out of control. Sometimes we're in such a spiritual slump that we just can't make it to functions where we'll see fellow Christians, so we say "I can't" and add an excuse. But excuses won't pull us out of that slump. Better to be honest and say, "I don't want to go and here's why."

In the parable of the two sons (Matthew 21:28-31), the one who said, "I don't want to work in the field," was easier to deal with than the one who said, "Sure, Dad. I'll go," then didn't. One could be reasoned with. ("It's gonna be yours someday. You wanna inherit something of value or a plot of dust?") The other? Who knew what was in his mind? How can you help someone when you don't know what's in his or her mind? How can people help themselves if they are more interested in excuses than action?

In the light of Philippians 4:13 I see my favorite phrase, "I can't," for what it most often is—a lie.

Father, help me to remember that I can more often than I can't. Help me not to hide behind excuses, but to be honest with You, myself and others. Change me from a woman who won't into a woman who will.

Chapter 19

I'm Sorry

"I'm sorry," Honey wailed as I approached with murder in my eyes. The talisman didn't work. This wasn't a first offense. "Don't just be sorry. Change your actions!" I stormed as I meted out punishment.

My daughter's sorrow didn't eliminate the punishment she feared. In fact, her sorrow disappointed me because I knew she wasn't sorry for her sin at all—only sorry that she'd been caught and would suffer.

That's rather discouraging, isn't it? whispered the Father.

"Yes," I agreed, still angry. "I know she isn't really sorry for what she did."

A sudden image sprang to mind—myself getting a traffic ticket. I had been so sorry—sorry I'd gotten the ticket, but not that I'd rolled through a stop sign. I had no money for a $50 ticket. How could I pay for this thing? What would my husband say?

What would have happened if I'd been going just a little faster and nosed somebody's car? What would the roads be like if everyone disobeyed the traffic laws? What did blithely breaking a traffic rule say about my character? I never asked myself those questions. My sorrow was like Cain's— strictly for myself.

I've learned there are two kinds of sorry: the David kind or the Saul kind.

First Samuel 15 tells us Saul's story. Saul was Israel's first king. God instructed him to destroy the pagan Amalekites completely along with everything belonging to them.

However, greedy Saul saved the best of the enemy nations' animals, and he saved the Amalekite king too as a living trophy. When Samuel, God's representative, entered the scene, he reprimanded Saul for disobedience and a rebellious attitude. That day the king lost his kingdom.

Was Saul sorry? You bet. He was sorry God was being so unreasonable. "I saved these animals to sacrifice," he argued. "What's so bad about that?"

God knew better. "He has turned away from me," He told Samuel (15:11). God knew Saul's heart. He knew that, even after Samuel's rebuke, Saul didn't mourn the poor spiritual example he had set. He wasn't sorry he'd failed God. He was only sorry for himself. And even as Samuel turned to go, Saul pleaded, "Please honor me before the elders of my people and before Israel . . ." (15:30). "Go to the worship service with me. Don't humiliate me before everyone. Don't let me lose face. Look at what this is doing to ME."

How different from the next king, David. We read about his famous sin in Second Samuel 11 and 12. David's response to God was nothing like Saul's: "I have sinned against the LORD" (12:13). He doesn't argue or rationalize. He expresses horror as he realizes the enormity of his sin.

I can tell when my children are appropriately sorry and when they're not. When "I'm sorry" is followed by the word "but," I know they have no true understanding of the wrong involved. "I'm sorry, but I thought . . ." or "I'm sorry but I didn't know . . ." It translates into "It's not really my fault." If "I'm sorry" is followed by excuses then I'm not really sorry. I'm saying the words only because I know that's expected of me.

Sometimes the words "I'm sorry but" are followed by rationalization. Again, these added phrases translate into, "I'm not really sorry." And they usually mean, "I'll do it anyway."

"I'm sorry" can mean "I feel bad." I may even feel badly for the right reason, but if I don't follow my sorrow with action, it becomes empty, meaningless.

In Bible biographies, real sorrow was always followed by a behavior change. To prove he was sorry that he tried to duck his mission, Jonah preached to the city of Ninevah. To prove he was sorry for denying his Lord, Peter gave the rest of his life in service to Christ and died a martyr. King David accepted his punishments with humility, acknowledging that he deserved them.

When my children are truly sorry, they follow the feeling with action. I see a change in attitude and behavior. When she was younger, Honey would make me a card or write me a note. When Junior has done something he knows is wrong, he is hardly consolable.

And what about Mom? The Father and I both know when I'm truly sorry too. I feel a horror at my sin, a sick melting feeling inside, and I know I deserve punishment. I am not concerned with my hide and don't desire to wriggle out of my punishment. I express no self-pity.

I'm truly sorry when I look at myself through the Father's eyes . . . when I read appropriate Scripture, when I think of the far-reaching repercussions of my actions and when I consider potential damage to my Christian witness or to another's faith. Then I am truly sorry. And then I'm willing to change.

True sorrow is painful, but only true sorrow brings real improvement. I don't want to cry "I'm sorry" just to avoid consequences any more than I want to see my daughter do it. I want to cry "I'm sorry" and mean it. I want to be sorry enough to change.

Chapter 20

Define: "Love"

hristmas Eve, 1990. The stockings were hung by the chimney with care, the Christmas cookies were baked and I had fa-la-la-ed around the house for days. A sleigh load of gaily wrapped boxes under the Christmas tree waited to be opened, and I was as excited about presents for me as I was about those for my children.

Soon we would walk up the road to my brother's house for a family celebration, complete with reading the traditional Christmas story and singing Christmas carols. Meanwhile, I puttered in the kitchen, putting final touches on my Christmas Eve fruit salad.

Twelve-year-old Honey had shopped earlier in the week and was showing off her purchases. She displayed a tablet adorned with kittens. "I was going to give it to you," she said, "but I decided to give it to Di-Di, instead."

"That's OK," I said. "I'm sure I'll like whatever you got me." Honey was silent, and I looked at her suspiciously. "You did get me something, didn't you?"

"No," she said slowly.

"No?"

She bit her lip. "I ran out of money."

I was shocked. My daughter had enough money to buy a present for her best friend, but not enough to get something for her own mother! Nothing! No small token for the woman who cleaned and washed and cooked for her, reminded her to change her underwear, helped her with her science project (never mind that as a result of my "help" she'd received a lower grade!).

I was a broken woman. (And I let my daughter know it!) Unable to face my family, I sent the kids and the fruit salad to their uncle's house and stayed behind to mourn.

"What's wrong?" asked Dad, thinking someone had died.

"Nobody bought me anything for Christmas!" I wailed.

"Nobody?" He looked at the Christmas tree.

"Honey bought a present for you and Junior and her best friend, and nothing for me." Now I was really hysterical. "She doesn't love me!"

"You know that's not true," he said. "I should have made sure the kids bought you something. We'll go get a present right now."

"It's not the same," I snapped.

I was right. Any present bought at this point

would be from Dad, not Honey. And I had wanted a present bought out of love, not pressure.

I wish I could say I was a perfect example of forgiveness and kindness and Christian charity—all the things that the season represented. But I wasn't. I nursed my grudge for the rest of the evening and when we opened presents the next morning, I made snide remarks. I was especially cruel when opening Junior's school-made goodie: "At least ONE of my children remembered their mother."

I had never thought of myself as manipulative, yet I was jerking my daughter around with a chain of guilt. And why? Because she'd been human.

Was it really Honey's fault she'd taken me for granted? And maybe she hadn't even taken me for granted, I reasoned. Maybe when she realized she had to bump someone from her Christmas list, she thought I'd be the one least offended. If so, that had certainly turned out to be an error in judgment.

As Christmas day ended, I wondered about my attitude toward my heavenly Parent. I had bought presents for family and friends and flung boxes of homemade candies at teachers and neighbors. I had remembered everyone—almost.

Where was the Father on my Christmas list? I hadn't attended the church's Christmas Eve service because it conflicted with my family's celebration. Christmas morning we'd ripped into our presents without even a prayer or a reading of the Christmas story. I remembered my daughter's phrase: "I ran out of money." Mine was: "I ran out of time." Hmmm.

"But Father, you know I love You," I protested. "I can't imagine my life without You at the center of it."

Any more than your daughter can imagine her life without you, said the Father gently.

Human love wants to sacrifice, wants to do right. Like Peter saying in John 21, "Lord, you know that I love you." Being a loving child and behaving like a perfect child are two different things. Love can't always be measured by gifts. Or by perfect behavior. The Father knows that. He lets me fail and still loves me, still works with me. He considers my attitude, my overall behavior.

I thought about the many cards and drawings my daughter had made for me through the years, the special notes I'd found sitting on my pillow or tucked into my computer keyboard. I'd enjoyed Christmas all year long for years and never realized it.

I thought about that very special birth we celebrate every year as a result of one very loving parent saying, "You have disappointed Me, My children. Yet I still love you. And here is My Gift to prove it."

So that is love: well-meant but less than perfect when strained through a human heart; understanding and sacrificial when coming from God's heart. I must follow the Father's example and show mercy and patience. And as I see how like my children I am, I must be thankful He is so very patient.

As yet another November appears on the calendar and Christmas goodies pop out on store shelves, Honey again counts her shekels and I remember Christmas day, 1990. That wasn't my merriest Christmas, but it was certainly the most important.

MOM'S LESSONS IN PHILOSOPHY

In my college philosophy course, I simply read ancient essays by Socrates and Plato and others. I often sat in class without a clue as to what was going on. Teachers and students debated in circular discussions that made me dizzy.

More is involved in philosophy than talking in circles, *said my heavenly Father.* So I'll let your children give you a few lessons.

PERSPECTIVE

Chapter 21

Up on the Roof

How toys can get on the roof of a suburban rambler is a mystery only the mother of small children can answer. I squinted through the summer sun. A collection of my children's favorite toys edged the house like goodies fallen from Santa's bag. "Please get them for us," begged four-year-old Honey.

"Oh, all right," I said. I fetched the ladder and propped it against the gutter. With determination I stepped on the bottom rung of the ladder and began to climb, chanting, "I'm not afraid. I'm not afraid." I scrambled onto the roof and tossed the treasures down to my children.

"It's not high," I told myself, and prepared to remount the ladder. But my body refused. *It is high*, I thought miserably, and sat down.

The children looked at me. "Come on down," called Honey.

"Not right now," I called back weakly. *Maybe never*, I thought.

I watched the children playing on the patio, Honey jumping rope and Junior riding his tricycle around the base of the ladder. I watched him going around and around and wondered if I would ever set foot on terra firma again. "Hi Mommy!" Junior called and waved.

I waved back, then crawled to the peak of the roof and surveyed the neighborhood. It was one of those rare afternoons when no one was home. No one. Someone was always around. I sighed. Was I doomed to be here all day?

A sudden happy thought occurred to me. My arranger was coming to work on some music. I consulted my watch. He was due in half an hour. He would rescue me! I settled down to wait for my rescue.

A half hour passed. Then an hour. I began to suspect that he'd either forgotten our appointment or had been detained.

Again, I surveyed the neighborhood. Still deserted. I looked at the ladder again. My husband wouldn't be home from work for a long time. Did I really want to be stuck on this roof all afternoon? My children were too young to be left on their own so long. No choice.

Like a swimmer testing the water, I stood and dipped an exploratory toe toward the ladder. Fingers of fear closed around my spinal column and I pulled my foot back. "I can't!" I wailed.

You can't, whispered my heavenly Father, *but I can. Step on the ladder. I won't let you fall.*

"I can't," I repeated, ready to sit back down.

Aren't you getting a little tired of being here?

"Of course," I said. "I'm getting a lot tired of being here."

Then don't let your fear keep you here. It is your fear, not Mine. My love is perfect, and it drives out fear. You were willing to trust another human. Trust Me. I'll be safer.

I bit my lip. "All right," I said. Again I moved toward the ladder, and the same fear grabbed me. I remembered a recent scene at the swimming pool. "Jump to Mommy," I had called. My son had jumped from the edge of the pool into my arms. I'd known he needn't fear. I'd catch him. Did the Father know He could keep me on that ladder?

Heart pounding, I stuck out my foot again and kept moving. I put a foot on the top rung, then put the other one beneath it. *That's right. Very good.*

Step by terrifying step, I descended the ladder. Each rung closer to the ground, I felt safer. Then I was finally off the ladder and vowing I'd never climb to the roof again.

But I have. My life, like everyone else's, involves a lot of roof-sitting. Most of the time, I have self-confidently climbed onto the roofs, thinking I could handle the situation ("We'll be able to pay for this car" . . . "I can handle this charge card" . . . "Motherhood will be a snap"). Then I find I am in a scary place, wondering how I would ever reach solid ground again. ("How can we pay for this car!" . . . "What do you mean the school can't pay your salary?" . . . "What's wrong with my child?")

My fears would like to keep me trapped, but they can't after I break free and put my foot on that first rung of the ladder. After I've taken those first scary steps, the rest of the trip is easy.

Like my literal rooftop experience, at times I've wished for a rescuer—someone to come and help me down. "I wish a rich relative would give me money so we could keep the car we couldn't afford . . . I wish someone would invent a miracle cure for my handicapped daughter . . . I wish I had a nanny."

No rich relative gave us the money to pay for the car we foolishly bought. We had to sell it. I had to cut up my charge card. ("Believe me," I told it, "this will hurt me more than it hurts you." How right I was!) As far as motherhood is concerned, no one invented a miracle to cure Dolly's handicap. No Mary Poppins appeared to carry me down from the scary pinnacle. I had to get on the ladder and descend to solid ground one parenting book, one mistake, one step at a time.

What have I learned about getting off roofs? How does one come to the point of making that first painful step? I'm not sure. What makes a small child "jump to Daddy" from a perch? Is it the knowledge that he'll be safely caught? What makes a soldier take risks during a battle? Is it the instinct that making an attempt and possibly experiencing victory is better than staying where he is?

When I have finally gotten so sick of being on that roof that I'd rather risk falling than stay up there any longer, when the lure of the happy

world below is too strong to resist, I can grit my
teeth, take a deep breath and stick my foot in the
direction of the top rung of the ladder.

The top rung is the hardest, the first step the
most difficult to make. But once my foot has
moved, I tell myself, "This is like childbirth. The
process has started. I can't turn back."

My friend, Candy, stuck on the roof of poverty
and unrealized dreams, moved to Nashville to
pursue her dream of being a songwriter. She knew
that first step of leaving family and friends would
be terrifying. But she also knew she had to take it.
The particular contacts she needed were in Nashville. Telling herself that the promise of success
outweighed the risk of failure and feeling the Father was leading her to her promised land, she put
her foot on the first rung of the ladder and decided
to leave the Pacific Northwest.

I watched Candy go down that ladder one rung
at a time: setting her departure date, calling moving companies, finding housing, making business
contacts. The transformation amazed me. She
seemed to gain new strength overnight. Candy
moved two years ago. Although her songwriting
dream has not yet come true, her business is
growing, she's happier than she's ever been and
she's glad she put her foot out in faith.

Like Candy, I've found that trip down the ladder may be a little nerve-racking. Or it may be a
lot nerve-racking, depending on how much I trust
my heavenly Father to catch me if I fall. Sometimes I have descended my ladder shaken and

with bruises that resulted from my own foolish-
ness. Sometimes getting down has been a breeze.
But I've always gotten down, eventually. I believe
I always will. "For he shall give his angels charge
over thee, to keep thee in all thy ways" (Psalm
91:11, KJV).

Chapter 22

The Debtors

"Twelve is a beastly age," I fumed as Miss Sour Lemon stormed out the door.

"Hurry back," I called sweetly after her.

The morning had started well until I asked Honey to brush her teeth.

"I brushed 'em, Mom," she protested.

And she had—for five seconds. "You need to do a better job," I said. "Please do it again."

"But I brushed them."

"Honey! Don't argue. Just go brush your teeth again."

"Mom. You don't understand. I brushed them already."

We left the bargaining table and went to war.

Granted, toothbrushing seems like a silly subject to squabble over, but a larger issue was at stake, and both of us knew it. So after the dust had settled from the first skirmish, I talked to my daughter about rebellion. I started the old, "You can make the next few years easy on yourself by obeying. Or you can be stiff-necked and rebellious and watch me turn mean and ugly" lecture. (If it was good enough for Doctor Dobson, it was good enough for me.)

"Now," I concluded, sure that we were finally on the same wavelength. "Why do you think I asked you to brush your teeth? Why would I care whether you brushed them well or not?" (I ask you fellow mothers, isn't the answer obvious?)

Honey missed the point. "Mom, I'd already brushed my teeth."

Hostilities broke out again.

After my beloved child left for school, I sat down, fuming, and made a "Sunday school lesson" for Honey, complete with quotes from Exodus 20:12 and Ephesians 6:1. I left a large space on the paper where my child could list the various things her parents had done for her: activities she'd enjoyed, outings we'd taken, the time we'd spent with her, the goodies we'd bought her.

Figuring she would conveniently remember little, I made my own list—easily filling a page, fuming as I wrote. After literally sacrificing our lives for her, what did we get in return? Ingratitude, rebellion, disrespect. We only wanted her to obey. Was that too much to expect?

I smugly finished my lesson. I knew when Honey tried to fill the space under the heading "What I Do for My Parents" it would be embarrassingly empty. "Hee, hee," I chortled.

Maybe Honey isn't the only one who should do this lesson, the Father suggested.

My smug smile faded. Surely the Father didn't think I was an ungrateful child. Did He? Was I?

I drew out a fresh piece of paper and listed the things my Father had done for me. I started with big things—salvation, joy, a great church, close family and good friends—and went all the way to little goodies, such as the cat given to our family complete with shots and neutering. The list was staggeringly long.

I poised my pen to write what I'd done for the Father. Compared to what He'd done for me, I knew my list would look about as impressive as my daughter's under "Things I Do for My Parents." I remembered the many times my devotions had resembled Honey's five-second toothbrushing session. I thought about the many times my own pleasure took precedence over pleasing God.

I looked at the final question on my daughter's lesson. It said, "What do my parents want me to do for them?" I sighed, for I knew the correct answer. For myself as well as for my daughter. "Does the LORD delight in burnt offerings and sacrifices as much as in obeying the voice of the LORD? To obey is better than sacrifice, and to heed is better than the fat of rams" (1 Samuel 15:22).

PERSPECTIVE, ADVANCED COURSE

Chapter 23

I Want to Do This

"Mom, can I go to Bedelia Beast's slumber party?" asked Honey.

Not Bedelia again, I thought. Bedelia was a bad influence who kept popping up in Honey's junior high life like a weed.

"Please?" Honey begged.

What American girl wouldn't want to attend a slumber party? And some of Honey's other friends would be there. But if I let Honey go, that would open the door to an undesirable friendship.

"Her mom will be there," said Honey.

I was not impressed. Surely Bedelia's mom had "been there" when Bedelia was growing up, but that hadn't affected Bedelia's behavior thus far.

I braced myself and said the ugly word no child wants to hear, followed by an explanation. I felt rotten, but Honey took it well.

Your daughter is setting a good example, observed my Father. *Do you know what I mean?*

I suspected what He meant, but I played dumb.

Over the past few years many "slumber parties" have tempted you, haven't they?

No sense denying it. I'd had many tempting invitations. Unlike my daughter, when an invitation came, I went without asking permission. And the Bedelia Beasts in my life definitely didn't have a good influence on me.

One slumber party I went to lasted for several years. It was during my Big Band era, when I sang in a country/variety band.

Like Honey, I looked for the reasons I should accept this invitation. It was an ideal job. I'd be doing something I loved—making music. I'd only work Friday and Saturday nights after the kids were in bed, and my husband would stay home with them, so I'd have no babysitting expenses. The money was great and would certainly come in handy. Even though I'd get home late on Saturday nights I could prop toothpicks in my eyes and go to church with the family on Sunday mornings.

Besides, my friend Country Corrie will be there, I reminded myself.

Some of my Christian friends were shocked. "We'll pray for you," they said.

"Give me a break," I snorted. "I'll only be in a country band. We're just playing in private clubs bearing the names of various animals. It's no big deal. Besides, maybe I'll get a chance to witness. After all, you can't introduce anyone to God just hiding in church all the time."

Very good arguments. And my job seemed perfect: good money, good music, good friends, good times—everything but good influence.

The perfect job turned out to be not so perfect. It sidetracked me from doing my favorite thing, songwriting. I spent all my spare time practicing with the band, playing with the band and promoting the band. I had no time left to write songs. And the hope of my material being performed never materialized.

Somehow I never got the opportunity to tell people about Jesus, either. Perhaps I blended in so well with the non-believers that no one could see anything different about me.

Over the next few years my faith remained strong, but my purity was slowly tarnished. It was such a gradual process that I didn't see it.

One night the band members sat around a table during our break, joking. A remark popped out of my mouth that, even today, years later, I would give anything to retract. In that instant I knew I was at the wrong "slumber party."

If I had been in a different environment would I have said that? I don't think so. "Bad company corrupts good character" (1 Corinthians 15:33). I learned that first hand.

Suddenly God's instruction to Israel in Exodus 34:15-16 made sense. I understood why He told them not to mingle with other nations.

They'll influence you, the Father cautioned. *You'll become close friends with them and association with them will slowly blind you and dull your conscience. Soon you'll condone things you never would have if you'd stayed separate.*

This was why I didn't want my daughter to become close with Bedelia Beast. Why hadn't I seen that this same principle also applied to me? Friends can influence us no matter what our age.

Looking back on that moment when I decided to become a paid musician, I don't remember hearing the Father say, "No. You can't do that." Of course, I don't remember ever asking Him about it. I just charged in.

Proverbs 14:12 says, "There is a way that seems right to a man, but in the end it leads to death." When my daughter was invited to Bedelia's slumber party, she could only see the good times, the food, the excitement. I didn't expect her to see the disadvantages of attending. How could she? She didn't have the experience and knowledge to see the possible repercussions. But she had a mother who could.

I've discovered that I don't always have the insight to know what's best for myself. Many things look good on the surface. Some things look like opportunities, when they may actually be sidetracks, pulling me from what I should really do. They may even damage my spiritual health.

Just because you're invited doesn't mean you go, the Father reminds me. How true.

I'll probably get many "slumber party" invitations in the future, and though some of those will be great parties, not all of them will be best for me or for my family.

Some issues are minor. It seems slightly silly to wonder if I'm in God's will when I take up quilting or play volleyball. But sometimes, though a hobby or activity isn't bad, it can take such a priority in my life and can so affect my spiritual growth and outlook that simply wanting to do it isn't reason enough.

Earlier, I developed a list of questions to ask before starting any activity. These questions revolved around time and talent. But now I have a new list of questions: What are the possible effects of this on my spiritual growth? Will I be a blessing or a curse to others? Will I be a good witness for Christ? Will this chip away at my faith or my purity? Is my associate's first goal to please God? Will I please God by doing this?

Sometimes I say, "This is important," when I really mean, "This is important to me." Those two statements are quite different. Not everything that seems important to me will be important for me, or even good for me. When I think something is important, I need to ask, "But will it be good for me? Will it be good for the others involved if I'm there? Most of all, will the Father be happy I'm doing this?" That's the bottom line.

The Good Parenting Rulebook says if you must deny a child something, offer him something else. The night of Bedelia's party, we let Honey have friends over, and she ended up being happier than if she'd been to the slumber party.

I realized the Father does the same thing for me.

Here. I know you love to sing. In this church, you can make music to your heart's content. See? You don't have to give it up completely. This is a party you can safely attend. It will make you strong spiritually.

Ask Me what you can do. I'll give you the insight to understand My Word and know what is good for you. I'll know what you're ready to handle. And if I don't let you attend one slumber party, I'll provide something else.

Maybe I've learned something from my daughter. Maybe now I see that even big girls need to ask permission before going to a party.

Chapter 24

What's Important?

Something was on my new rose-colored bedroom carpet that didn't belong. In only took a second for my brain to identify it. I looked at the cat with murder in my eyes.

She sat on my desk chair and stared at me, unconcerned. "The mess on the floor is your problem, not mine."

I disagreed with her. In fact, I did more than that. I scooped the princess off her perch and set her at the scene of the crime.

"Bad kitty," I scolded. I swatted her. "You are too young to have these problems," I called as she ran off to hide.

I glowered at my lovely rug and set to work. Grrrr. Cats!

After the carpet was clean, I felt badly about my outburst. I thought I had learned my lesson with the piano . . .

Moving day. One happy mover got the flu. Another was an hour late. But finally everyone arrived. I soon realized the Marx brothers were moving us. I murmured a silent prayer and left to sing at my nephew's wedding, hoping the moving men could manage without me. They did. Most of my worldly goods made it to storage, where they would stay while I pioneered in my island cabin, turning it into a house.

"Did the piano make it OK?" I asked Hubby later that day.

"It made it," he assured me.

A year and a half later, the family treasures came out of storage, including the old player piano, my inheritance, which I'd spent many hours refinishing. It was my pride and joy, my . . . well, you get the picture.

The bench came into the house first. It had a couple of little scratches.

"What's a scratch or two?" I said philosophically.

Then came the top of the piano, bearing a gash the size of the grand canyon. "Aaaaah," I screamed and fainted. (All right, so I didn't faint. I collapsed into the nearest chair and moaned.)

"It's only a scratch," said my husband. He could afford to be mature. His stereo speakers had survived perfectly.

"It's just a scratch." I repeated it like a litany. "It's only a thing."

Finally my message began to sink in. It was only a thing. Why did I attach so much sentimental value to an old player piano? My family had enjoyed some wonderful times at that piano, and so had my friends. But that didn't mean I had to forever preserve it as a monument to my past.

Player pianos, Dresden figurines, family china—these are all wonderful. But they're not invaluable, despite what antique experts say. However, the humans who live with these treasures are truly invaluable. When one of those possessions gets damaged, the real damage to worry about is the damage to the self-esteem of the one who broke it. And speaking of breaking . . .

When I was in grade school, I was at a girlfriend's, sewing campfire beads on Indian gowns. My friend's mom and dad were both at work, expected home within the hour. Her little brother was home and, like all little brothers, was being a pest.

I don't remember what he did to provoke me, but I remember what I did. I threw his baseball mitt at him. Not being terribly coordinated, I missed little brother and hit the ornate shell sitting on the mantelpiece. It crashed to the floor, and my heart fell too—right into my stomach.

"Don't worry," little brother told his sister. "I'll tell Dad that Sheila did it."

"Sheila did it." Oh, boy. Sheila had indeed done it. I felt terrible. This thing probably cost a fortune. What had I done? And more to the point, what would my best friend's parents do to me? I waited for THE PARENTS to return with every vital organ twisted and knotted.

Time dragged. Then, suddenly, they were home. They were getting out of the car, coming up the walk. *Dear God, I am so sorry. Help me!*

My friend's father was barely in the door before
little brother informed him of the damage I'd
done. The father (who had always made me a little nervous) grew another ten inches. His face red-
dened. He glared at me and roared, "Way to go,
Sheila. That was an expensive shell. . . ." More followed. I don't remember it. I only remember the
tone of his voice and my own horror at what I'd
done, fear for my life and misery over the fact that
I only had a dollar in my piggy bank.

After growing up, I remembered that incident
and realized that what got broken wasn't invaluable or irreplaceable. What was invaluable was a
child's feelings. Those had been ignored. The first
concern had been for the object.

Have I been guilty of doing the same thing?
Often. But I hope I'm getting better at putting
"things" in perspective. Different incidents have
helped me learn to shrug my shoulders and say,
"Oh well." Incidents like: oven cleaner, mistaken
for furniture polish, sprayed (by me!) on the din-
ing room table; a kitchen table leaf cracked off
during a game of spoons; or a laughing guest falling onto the couch and breaking it.

Surely if our possessions were so precious we
could take them with us when we leave this
world. Obviously, since we all depart without
them, they're not necessary. And if they're not
necessary, when one is accidentally broken or
stained, how upset should we become?

We all tend to attach sentimental value to our
possessions: "This was my mother's." "My hus-

band gave me that for our first wedding anniversary."

Of course, nothing is wrong with enjoying those gifts of love, but a fine line lies between taking pleasure and turning those tokens into icons. A thing is not sacred. It's wrong to elevate our possessions to the same level as those who give them to us.

When accidents happen, I need to train myself to ask, "Was that prize temporal or eternal?"

The next question on my pop quiz should be, "What will be the long-range effect of this loss?" If a favorite knickknack or dish gets broken will anyone really care in 100 years? How about fifty? Ten? Two?

When I look at the person responsible for the breakage and compare him or her to the shattered item, I must instantly decide: Which is more important? (With my piano, I took quite a few minutes to come to the right conclusion!)

I guess I'll never advocate careless disregard for our goodies. Not caring for items smacks of ingratitude. So my kids still get in trouble when they disobey rules and play ball in the living room and break something. But, as my mother used to say, accidents happen—to kids and maybe to amateur furniture movers too. Yeah, and probably even to cats.

Chapter 25

Just A Minute!

"**M**om, can I have the Scotch tape?" asked nine-year-old Junior.

At the age of nine, why couldn't Junior simply find the tape himself? After Junior and Honey used three rolls in three days and I had to wrap a birthday present with masking tape (this does not look pretty), I hid the tape in my desk drawer and rationed it.

When Junior made his request, I was applying makeup and had on half an eye. "Just a minute," I called.

"Mom, I need it right now."

"Just a minute. May I please finish what I'm doing first?"

My son didn't answer. Instead he drifted to his room to pace. I knew if I wasn't done in fifty-nine seconds, he'd return.

This is so typical, I thought. *Junior has no patience. Of course I would never act that way with my heavenly Father . . .*

"Please, Father, end this unemployment stuff right now" . . . "Will you heal Dolly this second, while I'm here? Right now. I want to see a miracle this second" . . .

I will take care of this, promises my Father.

"When?" I pester. "Now?"

Soon. When the time is right.

"The time is right," I insist. "I can't think of a better time for You to drop everything and do what I want."

My son can't think of a better time for me to drop everything and do what he wants either. Never mind how I feel about it or what I think is best. Junior is, like most children, self-absorbed. When he wants something he sees little else.

I know I'll eventually help him. I also know it doesn't hurt him to wait. In fact, waiting is good for him. It's an exercise in faith and self-control— a chance for him to learn patience.

Besides, some things, by nature, take time. When Junior wants ginger cookies he must understand a process is involved for me to produce those cookies. I must gather the ingredients and mix them into dough. The dough must be rolled into balls and baked. The process involves an unchangeable amount of time.

Sometimes I get hungry for my own kind of ginger cookies. But I forget about the baking process preceding the warm cookie. If I want a new kitchen, I must remember that any remodeling project will take time. I have to suffer through dust and upheaval before I can have those new counters and cupboard. Losing weight is not an instant accomplishment. It takes time to discipline myself out of those extra pounds. No one will hand me a magic knife to instantly slice off the unwanted fat. I have to endure the process.

Nothing fuels my temper faster than getting stuck in traffic. "When will this mess move?" I mutter. "If I have to crawl along like this much longer I'll crawl out of my skin!"

A child asks me the same question and I snap, "We'll move when we move!"

I can do nothing to speed up a traffic jam. But I can do something to slow down my quick temper. I can play twenty questions with the kids while we wait for traffic to move. We can sing camp songs. We can play memory games. These entertain us and distract us from irritating circumstances.

When traveling, we've learned to take along favorite books or portable video games. Even on short trips. We've found over the years that you never know what might happen.

If I'm stuck alone in traffic, I try to distract myself from frustration by contemplating a new idea, singing, planning menus for the week or listing chores for the following day. If I keep a small tablet in my purse, waiting time in traffic or at the doctor's office isn't such a strain on my patience. Instead, I can remain happily (or semi-happily) employed.

My friend Lorian doesn't have time for leisure reading between her job and her family responsibilities, so she always carries a book in her purse.

She claims she's read many books by just taking advantage of spare minutes.

When I want cookies, I can help myself wait through the baking process by planning and anticipating. "When I finally lose that ten pounds, I'll buy a new dress" . . . "When I escape this traffic snarl and get home I'll take a bubble bath, then pop a frozen pizza in the oven for an easy meal."

Since I was raised in the shadow of golden arches and gifted with charge card privileges from an early age, I grew up believing instant gratification is wonderful. I've felt I should have instant gratification in other areas of my life as well. "I want to be a great teacher and a famous writer," I used to beg. "Now. So what if I'm only twenty-three? I've always known I was destined for greatness, just like Joseph. Why can't You use me now, Lord?"

You're not ready yet, said the Father. *You need to live, to fail and succeed. You need some experience. You also need to pay your dues.*

Like my son in a baseball game, I was anxious to be at bat, to make my home run, to have my moment in the sun, to do great things for God. . . .

"My husband wants to do great things too," I'd continue. "I want him to do great things. Right now. After all, he isn't getting any younger. When can my husband teach adult Sunday school? When can he be associate pastor? He's ready right now. And so am I."

"Don't push and manipulate for what you want," our adult Sunday school teacher advised during class. "Don't worry about cultivating the right people who can get you that position teaching Sunday school or leading worship. Serve in small ways and let God open the doors for you. If it's His will, He'll see that they open at the right time." Good advice for me.

Patience is a mark of spiritual maturity. Hebrews 10:36 and 12:1 agree that it's a struggle being a Christian in a pagan world. It seems like everyone gets ahead but me. Come to think of it, it's a struggle in the church too. It seems like everyone but me is progressing spiritually.

You'll finish the course, says the Father. *Run the race with patience. Keep plugging away.*

"How long do I have to suffer this tribulation?" I wail.

Until it's over, comes the reply.

"But we also rejoice in our sufferings, because we know that suffering produces perseverance; perseverance character" (Romans 5:3-4).

Do I rejoice in my sufferings? Am I patient and persevering? I look at my son and realize that I'm not much farther along in learning patience than he is.

In difficult circumstances, I have to keep moving. I can't stop to demand that the finish line be moved closer to me. I have to continue running, living Hebrews 12:11. I have to meet each new trial as if it were one more exciting hurdle on a lifelong race course. I must keep my eyes on the goal and know I'll reach the end of the race when I reach the end of the race. No sooner. Meanwhile, I must keep breathing and running, putting one foot down, then the other. I must keep going to church. I must keep reading my Bible. I must keep trying to maintain my spiritual and emotional health.

"You need to preserve so that when you have done the will of God, you will receive what he has promised" (Hebrews 10:36).

I will receive what God has promised when I have done His will. That phrase "the will of God" includes a lot and requires a lot. It implies a long gestation period.

God's kingdom is not like a fast food chain. Instant gratification is not the goal. The goal is development and perfection, ending in eternal gratification for the Father and myself and my Christian family.

Finally finished with my face, I said, "Now I'll get you the tape, Junior."

Ah, tape at last!

I envisioned myself in the future, just as thrilled when the Father pulls an answered prayer from a huge heavenly desk. *Here, daughter. I told you I'd get this for you.*

Junior ran off with his prize, excited to get to work, his agonizing wait for the tape now an unpleasant memory.

I watched him go and knew I'll be the same way someday when those things I thought I needed so urgently are taken care of. I smiled, comforted, took another deep breath and prepared to run another mile.

Chapter 26

The Kamikaze Kid

Junior didn't walk at nine months. He ran. And he's been running since then—into crowds where he'd do a vanishing act David Copperfield couldn't top, down the supermarket aisle and out of sight, over the fence and down the street.

When he wasn't running he was climbing: to the top of a swingset when he was three, to the very top of tall trees when he was seven. *What's left?* I would ask, *The Empire State Building? Mount Everest?*

When Junior was five we all accompanied Dad to the airport as he left for a three-week trip to Germany. Junior and Honey went in with him and the other travelers to the concourse while I kept Dolly and went to park the car.

I parked and, pushing Dolly in her wheelchair, headed for the concourse. From a distance I heard the wail of a child in pain. *Some poor mother has her hands full*, I thought sympathetically.

As I neared Gate B, the wail grew louder and more familiar. Dad greeted me, towing a bloody, berserk Junior, who had tried to vault a metal railing and was now toothless. Some poor mother certainly did have her hands full. We said a quick goodbye to Dad and spent the rest of our evening in the dentist's office.

Of course, that was just one of many delightful experiences. One New Year's Day Junior put a hole in the roof of his mouth with a cardboard horn left over from New Year's Eve. Another time, he jumped off the ten-foot fence. He also engineered the amazing "turn your eye into an egg" bicycle feat. . . . You get the picture.

Junior next entered gymnastics, the perfect outlet for all that energy and daring. And the perfect place to break his neck.

I'd watch him swing from rings that seemed at least fifteen feet off the ground, or son poised in midair, arms and legs taut, toes pointed, and try not to remember all the stories I'd heard about gymnasts winding up in wheelchairs.

When Operation Desert Storm was raging, I worried about future wars. "If they initiate the draft again, I'll take Junior to Canada," I vowed. "I didn't raise my son to be sacrificed on the field of battle. How could I bear it? How could I stand to lose him?"

Suddenly, I realized the same thing that has probably dawned on every other Christian mother at some time or other: This is the sacrifice the Father made! How hard He must have found it to send a part of Himself to earth, watch it develop into a Man—not just any man, but a perfect Man—knowing that Son's future. This was the ultimate risk.

The Father sent His only Child to the greatest war of all and let Him die. He let that Child be abused and tortured. All for me. Such incomprehensibly unselfish love! Could I do that for anyone? No way.

My children are my greatest treasure. I want to hoard them for myself. With one child severely handicapped, the thought of seeing my remaining two even slightly damaged is too horrible to contemplate. I ask myself, *What good could possibly justify the hurt and suffering of my child? For what cause could I give him or her up?* And my honest answer is, *None.*

Jesus Christ was the Father's greatest treasure, and He spent that treasure to ransom His captive creation. I can't even begin to understand a love so great. Thinking about my children and how I feel about them, I believe I can, at least, begin to appreciate it.

Chapter 27

He Flies through
the Air

Sitting in the audience at a gymnastics competition and watching Junior hurtle through space and land in a heap on the floor was like being in a horror movie. I gasped as he screeched with pain. The other mothers held me back while Junior writhed on the floor and the medics rushed to his aid.

What I had feared ever since Junior took up this high-risk sport had finally happened. My baby had been badly injured. I held my breath and waited to break lose from my friends' restraining grasp. Junior was already embarrassed over blowing his event and wailing like a banshee, but I wanted to run to his side and embarrass him even more.

The wound, it turned out, wasn't too serious— only a dislocated elbow. Considering he could have dislocated his neck, this was good news.

I should have considered it good news when Junior announced several weeks later that he was quitting gymnastics. But I didn't. By now I'd become a true gymnastic mother. I was sure my son would one day be on a platform, receiving a gold medal. And he would throw all that away because of one mishap? "Quit?" I stammered.

"Quit?" echoed his coach. "But he was doing so well."

"Quit?" echoed another gymnastics mom. "He had so much potential."

"So much potential," I sighed, and saw a future college scholarship fly away. In vain I encouraged my son to reconsider. After investing so much time and money, and with such a talent, quitting seemed like such a waste.

But this was his decision to make.

"You can't force him to be in the gym," said one coach. "He'd be afraid, and the fear would make him hesitate. Then he could really get hurt."

So I let Junior exercise his free will. I saw the benefits of continuing the sport: good discipline, great exercise and body toning, ah yes, and that college scholarship. But Junior saw pain and fear and said, "No."

Honey is also exercising free will a lot these days. I've given her all kinds of great career suggestions, but Honey prefers to choose her own course. I'm proud my daughter wants to be a police officer, but if I were choosing, she'd plan something much safer.

Actually, Honey's big decisions, such as her choice of future career, don't bother me as much as some of her smaller, current decisions. I long to see her demure in dresses and makeup, surrounded by male admirers. Right now she's surrounded by boys, but because she's one of them. Honey scorns makeup and lace, preferring jeans and t-shirts. I can only get her to dress like a female to go to church.

I look at my tall, beautiful daughter and say, "She could be a model." I sigh and shake my head. "I don't know why my children won't listen to their mother when she knows what's best for them."

Perhaps it's because they are creatures of free will, whispers the Father. *This makes them unique and interesting.*

"They would be just as interesting if they always did what I wanted," I mutter.

If they always did what you wanted they would be robots, the Father says. *Because they have free will, their cooperation, when it comes, is sweeter, their love is more precious.*

I think about a garden. And a tree. And a woman who exercised her free will and chose disobedience.

Then I think of myself, Eve's daughter. How alike we are. Eve must have loved the Father, the One who gave her life. And yet, for just a moment she thought she knew what was best for herself, thought she knew better than her heavenly Parent. And I, like my children, also often think I know what I'm doing. "This is a wise choice," I say. "I'm free to choose, and this is what I choose."

The Father, who knows what is best, says, *Are you sure?*

"Yes," I say, "I'm sure." Like Eve, I choose. I reach. Sometimes what I pick is good, sometimes it isn't.

The Father says, *I want you to do what I know is best, but you're right. The choice is yours.*

I learned that a former gymnast can make good use of skills in the sport of diving. I suggested Junior give it a try, and he's now happily flying through the air and landing in water, not on solid ground. Somehow this seems safer. Junior is happy and so am I.

You're still guiding him, says the Father. *Just as I continue to guide you, even when the choices you make are not the ones I want.*

I have a revelation. "Growth is continuing, isn't it, Father? And wrong decisions can affect us adversely. But we can learn from them. And You can still guide us and make us what You want us to be in spite of our free will."

Your free will is My greatest trial, says the Father, *and your greatest blessing.*

I watch my son fall like an arrow from the high dive and pierce the water. He also shows great talent in this sport. He faces the opportunity for great success if he chooses to reach for it. He may also choose to discard this opportunity. How he uses his free will can affect his future.

And that's only one area of his life where he

will use his free will. He'll face decisions that, if made foolishly, will be far more costly than the choice about what sport to play.

I think of a friend whose children's choices have brought hard consequences. One child is a teenage mother. Another is in prison. But their mother forgives all, working with them right where they are. Her children's choices have grieved her deeply, but she walks with them on the hard road they've taken, encouraging them to learn from their mistakes.

How hard it must be for the Father to watch us make wrong choices. Our greatest gift can also be our greatest curse.

Oh, Father, I'm not sure my son is ready for that gift. I'm not sure I am, either. Help us both use it wisely.

PRINCIPLES
OF
CHANGE

Chapter 28

Did You Brush
Your Teeth?

Six-year-old Junior is bouncing around in his jammies, ready for bed. "Did you brush your teeth?" I ask.

"Oops!" He bounces to the bathroom.

Ten-year-old Junior appears at the dinner table with hands that look like they could sprout seeds. "Did you wash your hands?"

"Oh, Mom," he moans and disappears into the bathroom.

"Did you brush your hair?" "Did you make your bed?" "When was the last time you went to the bathroom?" "Have you started your homework?" "Did you put on clean underwear?" When will it end? When will they finally do these things on their own?

The answer: eventually, when I've nagged an uncountable number of times over an indefinite number of years. Just when I think it's hopeless, my son will come to the table with clean hands. My daughter will have a home of her own, a clean home. (Oh, Lord, I believe. Help Thou my unbelief!) Through forced repetition those actions, once so hard to remember, will have become habits.

Like my children, I too have spent several years trying to master important habits.

First was the good eating habit, which I worked so hard to instill in my children, but ignored for myself. It all began with the Big "D."

When I delivered my seven-pound son, I was left with thirty-five extra pounds that refused to leave with the baby. It was time to go on a . . . (grit the teeth!) diet. I'd never dieted in my life and my eating habits were sloppy and indulgent. And I liked them that way, thank you. Unlike many women, who have an emotional cause for an ongoing weight problem, I can only point to self-indulgence and gluttony.

But I didn't like my extra chin or the forearms that bulged, not with muscle, but with fat. So I joined a Christian version of Weight Watchers, complete with weekly Bible study and weigh-in. If that weren't enough, I decided to start some serious form of exercise too. I wanted to look like my friend Gorgeous Greta, who taught aerobics, so I signed up for Greta's aerobics class.

The first day of class I showed up at the gym, looking like a vision in my white maternity shorts and black tights—all I had that fit! Everyone else in the class was dressed in coordinated Jane Fonda designer outfits, complete with cute leg warmers. I felt slightly uncomfortable.

But that was nothing compared to how I felt when the music started and the Barbie dolls came to life. Everyone knew the steps. They all knew how to do the rocking horse and the step-glide, or whatever it was. And they all did it with energy. I was panting. Wasn't it getting warm in here?

The nightmare continued and I hopped and skipped and tripped around the room, trying to keep up. My heart hammered. My head pounded so hard I felt it would explode any minute. Greta had said aerobics was fun. Greta had lied. This wasn't fun. This was work. No, work wasn't even the right word. This was torture!

The first week on my diet I had severe withdrawals. I dreamed of M&M's and ice cream. I lusted after bread. I was hungry and cranky.

But my friends helped. "Are you ready to go to aerobics?" chirped my neighbor, who had signed up to take the class with me and to offer moral support.

"We'd better not have another taco," said Bitty Betsy diplomatically, pretending to be full after one scrawny little shell half-filled with a table-spoon of meat and some lettuce. My husband helped too. "Are you in the ice cream?"

"Nag, nag, nag," I grumbled. "Is this how my children feel when I keep after them?"

Three months and thirty pounds later I had formed new habits. After three months of agony, of repeatedly making myself think about what was going into my mouth and why, I was finally eating properly and without anyone nagging me. Amazing! The more I used my will power the more I had. My will was like a muscle needing to be exercised. As I applied the weights to it and worked it, it's strength increased.

I also endured a long, hard attempt to master tennis. Every time I hit the ball over the fence, I wondered why I wanted to play that stupid game. Countless balls hit against the wall—follow through, let the ball bounce lower before you hit it, don't tip the racquet face up.

How badly do I want to play this dumb game? Concentrate. Try again. I did it! Oops! That time I missed. Try again. Got it right two times in a row. Concentrate. Try again. How many hundred strokes had my friend-coach said it takes before this becomes a habit?

We won't say how many years it's taken me to get where I am today. Nobody's invited me to Wimbledon yet, but I can play a pretty mean game for an amateur. At my age, that's good enough.

How about when I struggled to establish my quiet times? How often the Father had to whisper, *Are you going to get up? It's time.* Or, *Have you read My Word today? Why don't you get out your Bible and do that now?* Every day it was a battle to ignore that newspaper and kitchen mess and go to a quiet corner with my Bible. Many times I lost the battle. Forming a new habit required Herculean effort and discipline. It was so difficult to be consistent.

That's how it is when you're forming new habits. It is difficult to be consistent. Success must be preceded by a certain amount of failure. Otherwise it wouldn't be success. You'd have nothing with which to compare it.

Part of the problem is that the human heart does not naturally enjoy discipline. But God expects us to bring some measure of willingness to our spiritual fitness plan. Ephesians is full of phrases like, "Walk worthy," "Be subject," "Do not," and "Put on," as in "Make an effort, children."

When we make the initial effort, the Father gives us strength to succeed (Phililippians 2:13). But we must start the process. If we just come to the gym, He'll be our trainer. And He'll stay with us as we sweat and work and strengthen our spiritual muscles. He won't do the sit-ups for us because He knows that won't make us strong. But He will work with us. He'll do His part. He'll make sure the change takes place. But we have to do our part. We have to make a habit of getting to the gym every day for the workout.

I've read that it takes twenty-one days to form or break a habit. I believe that. And when it involves spiritual matters, I believe it takes longer: twenty-one months, twenty-one years.

But when we make the effort, it does eventually happen somewhere along the way. Sometimes it happens so subtly that you can't write in your journal and point to as "this is the day I got it together." One day you look at yourself and notice a change,

just as one day you realize you don't have to nag
your son to brush his teeth or wash his hands, just
as one day you look in the mirror and see your two
chins have become one and a half. Somewhere along
the way what you struggled to master has become a
habit and your life is different because of it.

I realize our spiritual walk should be more than
a habit. But I think habit is, and should always be,
part of our spiritual life. After all, habits can be
good. Personal hygiene habits protect us from dis-
eases. Study habits produce good grades. Spiritual
habits help protect us from spiritual disease.

Nothing is wrong with going to church "out of
habit." Church was a family habit when I was a
child. In fact, it was so much a part of my life that
it remained so when I hit my teens and changed
from habit to way of life. My social world centered around the church youth group and I loved
it.

And today, going to church and Sunday school
are as much a habit for Honey and Junior as
brushing their teeth. When they were little, they
went to church with Mom and Dad because it was
what we did every Sunday. Now they're involved
in youth group activities and their teenage years
center around church.

Scripture promises us that this training will pay
off. First our children go with us to worship God
out of habit. One day they will go out of love.

My devotions are a habit. Just like my writing. I
don't always feel in the mood to be creative when
I sit to write a novel, but because my imagination

supplements our income, I habitually sit at my computer every day. As I write, I become involved in the story. The more involved I become, the more excited I get about what I'm doing.

I have the same experience concerning my Bible study. I'm not always in the mood. I'm mentally distracted and I don't expect to get anything out of what I'm doing. But once I've gotten involved, I make personal applications and get excited about what I'm learning.

At times, I may not walk away with earth-shattering revelations, but habit keeps me coming back. Even if one time I am not caught up in a rapturous experience, the next time I might be. And no matter what my emotions are doing, every time I study the Word, I learn.

Prayer time isn't always emotional fireworks, either, but neither is every conversation I have with my husband. I don't let that keep me from bending his ear. In fact, I've realized that in a marriage, although the "How'd you sleep?" conversations are just habit, they're important because they're rooted in love and keep alive the feeling of security and comfort and oneness in the relationship.

My habit prayers, like "Please watch over my family today," are as important to my relationship with my Father as the major, emotional prayers. They are a part of the fabric of my relationship with my Father.

Simply knowing I should do something doesn't mean I do it consistently, any more than knowing how to play tennis makes me a good player. I ac-

quire skill on the tennis court through time and effort. Just like maturity. But as I struggle to master
good spiritual habits, I remind myself that spiritual growth is not behavioral science. I'm not like
the rat in the maze who, once he learns how to get
the cheese, will be constant in his behavior. I'm
complex and I'm human. That's why spiritual
growth is a miracle—every inch of it!

Like physical growth, it's hard to know exactly
when those spiritual changes happened. You look
at your child one day and realize he's taller. You
look at yourself and realize you've changed. One
day your child apologizes to a sibling without any
prompting from Mom.

I remember the times I nagged my son to wash
his hands and brush his teeth. Suddenly I don't
have to any more. I take comfort. Maturity is coming. I have hope, for my children and myself.

Chapter 29

Have You Seen Pictures of My Children?

Eddie Elder approached me at church one day and said, "I've got to tell you about your daughter."

Oh, no, I thought and braced myself for the worst. "She did something that took guts," Eddie continued, and told me about my daughter's thoughtful act.

Suddenly the buttons on my blouse strained against the buttonholes as my chest swelled, and my hat was beginning to fit snugly. I looked across the church at Honey and smiled. Such a good kid.

I had the same thoughts when Junior came home from school camp. He'd only been gone three days, but I was sure he'd grown an inch. He looked so big for ten. Was his voice changing? I peeked into his bedroom that night and admired my sleeping son. Such a handsome boy! And so sweet! I beamed on my innocent-looking child. Watching that darling, dreaming face, who would suspect that this was the little boy who got into trouble for punching another sweet little boy on the school playground only a week earlier?

Go to any high school reunion and you'll see men and women displaying plasticized pictures of children with big smiles and tiny teeth, or smiles with teeth that seem too big for their mouths, or smiles with few teeth.

"That's Ginny. She's president of her fourth grade class," brags Dad. "And here's Michael. He's a natural on the ball field."

"Straight A's," another mom says. "This is the third year in a row."

Of course, these parents aren't telling you that Miss Straight A's has a fat head to go with her terrific grades and a tendency to bully her little brother. And that father with the son who's such a great ball player has to fight with him every day to do his chores.

So why don't we list our children's faults when talking about them? Maybe pride is involved. No one likes to say, "Hey, my child is a disaster and I'm a failure as a parent."

But I think it's more than that. I think when we see our children we look with eyes of love, we see what's good.

Thanks to this intimate exposé, all who know me will know my children, like their mother, are flawed. But when I'm talking with an acquaintance about them, I don't usually discuss their flaws. (I save my grumbling for my good friends, who already know my children aren't perfect.) I like to brag about my son's athletic abilities, his sensitivity and his sanguine disposition. I boast about my daughter's beauty and artistic ability and her thoughtfulness. (Want to see the cute keychain with the little tennis ball that she bought me at the mall with her own money last week? Do you think she's still trying to make up for that Christmas blunder so many years ago? Just kidding, Honey!)

I think I know why I'll tell anyone who will listen how spiritually sensitive and mature both of my darlings are, illustrating with stories of noble deeds and sacrifices. It's because I see their character in the making. I see the good, mature people they're becoming. And that's exciting! Like watching a work of art in progress.

When God commended Job to Satan, He knew the man wasn't perfect. But he knew Job's heart. God knew Job loved Him and He knew what Job was becoming.

I guess that's why I'm so quick to commend my children. I see them blooming into something lovely, something that pleases me, that gives me hope that they will be a credit to their parents and to their heavenly Father. I see them trying to be kind and thoughtful. I see them trying to obey. I see them reaching and growing, and I am pleased.

Even Dolly, our oldest, born into a society that often measures human worth by a person's usefulness and accomplishment, has great value in my eyes. I see a usefulness the world doesn't recognize. The Dollys of this world, the handicapped and the helpless, jerk us out of our selfishness and demand we care for others. They make us think beyond our own wants. I look at Dolly's sweet spirit and her happy face and her little button nose and wonder how anyone could help but love her.

As I delight in watching my children grow and mature, I can almost feel the Father's hand on my shoulder, watching with me and saying, *Yes, that's how I feel about you, too. I'm still changing you. We're going from glory to glory* (2 Corinthians 3:18), *from mercy to mercy. I look at you and with love, I see a child washed clean. I see what you are becoming and what you will become. I know you have flaws, but I specialize in transforming flawed people* (just read the Old Testament). *Knowing your weaknesses doesn't kill My love for you any more than knowing your children's faults kills your love for them. I planned for you. I have always taken an interest in you. I love you, child.*

Thanks, Father. I'm learning.